UPROOTING
ANGER

UPROOTING
ANGER

BIBLICAL HELP FOR A COMMON PROBLEM

ROBERT D. JONES

PUBLISHING
P.O. BOX 817 • PHILLIPSBURG • NEW JERSEY 08865-0817

Page design and typesetting by Lakeside Design Plus

Printed in the United States of America

Library of Congress Cataloging-in-Publication Data

Jones, Robert D., 1959–
    Uprooting anger : biblical help for a common problem / Robert D. Jones.
        p. cm.
    Includes bibliographical references and index.
    ISBN-10: 1-59638-005-5 (pbk.)
    ISBN-13: 978-19638-005-9 (pbk.)
    1. Anger—Religious aspects—Christianity. 2. Anger—Biblical teaching. I. Title.

BV4627.A5J67 2005

        2005049438

CONTENTS

ACKNOWLEDGMENTS

Acknowledgments can read like Old Testament genealogies: if you're not listed, you might skip to something more exciting. But my acknowledgments, like Old Testament genealogies, serve an important function: they remind us of real people whom God knows and uses.

I thank God for the dear church congregation I served from 1985 until the summer of 2004, before relocating to teach biblical counseling at Southeastern Baptist Theological Seminary. Grace Fellowship Church, of Hurricane, West Virginia, and my former fellow elders, Gerald, Fred, Dave, Allen, and Danny, provided their senior pastor with ongoing opportunities to study, minister, and write over our eighteen years together. This book sprang initially from a series of sermons on anger, and I doubt I'll ever forget the body for whom they were first prepared.

For nearly as many years, through their writing, lecturing, and private discussion, the teaching faculty of the Christian Counseling and Educational Foundation in Glenside, Pennsylvania, have stimulated my biblical thinking. David Powlison's lectures, writings, and chapter-by-chapter advice and oversight of my earlier doctoral project were invaluable. Thank you, David, Paul Tripp, Ed Welch, and John Bettler, for teaching me how to uproot sinful anger from my life. My wife also thanks you for giving her a better husband than I was before I met you.

Many of us pastors and professors have appreciated P&R's longtime commitment to biblical counseling; I am privileged to team with them to add another offering to our movement's growing body of Christ-centered, practical literature. Thank you, Al Fisher, for opening this door, and Tara Davis for managing the project, and me, with skill and grace.

Earlier versions of two chapters first appeared in booklet form. Thank you, Sue Lutz of CCEF, for your editorial touches and for encouraging me to keep writing.

This book did not arise in intellectual isolation. I am grateful to the many dozens of pastors, fellow church members, and counselees who have interacted with me on the subject of anger and have given me opportunity to counsel and teach them. Entrusting your lives to me has driven me to search the Scriptures to bring Christ into your struggles. In the following pages, your names and identifying details have been changed to protect the not-yet-glorified.

My wife, Lauren—my lover and best friend for more than twenty-two years—helped me in all the ways mentioned above, and many more. Along with our sons, Tim and Dan, she gracefully handled my anger displays and patiently endured my long hours on the laptop. Over the years the truths in this book have helped us to learn together how to resolve marriage conflicts and repent of anger in our family life.

INTRODUCTION

Grandma Kresge was right. I didn't admit it at the time; teenage stubbornness balked at doing so. But as an adult, I now concede. "Bobby," she said, "you've got to get the weeds by the roots, or they'll just grow back." Unfortunately, Grandma was right. Dandelion fields forever.

Years later as a newlywed, I remembered Grandma's words. Our retired neighbor, who in my judgment had too much time on his hands, maintained a manicured lawn. While he never knew my grandmother, he knew the truth she preached: get the roots, or the weeds will return. Every day he uprooted those intruding dandelions. The result was a weed-free yard.

What do these lawn-care reflections have to do with anger? Simple: you must uproot your sinful anger, or its weeds will return. There will be no thorough and lasting godly change without root removal. Moralistic efforts to be patient with your coworkers won't cut it. Regret-riddled resolutions to stop yelling at your kids won't last. You must rip out those angry roots.

THE BIBLE AND OUR ANGER PROBLEM

Is uprooting sinful anger a realistic goal? Can it happen? God's answer in the Bible is "Yes!" This book is about The Book, the Bible, and what it teaches us about anger.

In one sense, the Bible is all about anger. Consider the patriarchs in Genesis or the Israelites sojourning in Exodus. Observe
the relational dynamics in Judges and Samuel and Kings. Enter
the struggles of the psalmists. Heed the wisdom and warnings
of Proverbs. Feel the passion of the prophets. Listen to our
Lord in the gospels. Watch King Herod's royal rage erupt. See
the interplay between Jesus and the Jewish leaders. Hear the
apostle Paul counsel his congregations. Humble yourself before
Peter's and James's piercing reproofs. From cover to cover, in
narrative and precept, the Bible is a Book about anger.

While this reality sobers us, it also breeds hope. Why?
Because this Book about anger gives answers for that anger!
Scripture generates hope for angry people like us. This is wel-
come news because, as seasoned counselors know, nearly every
relational conflict involves anger issues. God's Word gives us
all that we need to handle this universal problem. "All Scripture is God-breathed and is useful for teaching, rebuking, cor-
recting and training in righteousness" (2 Tim. 3:16). "His
divine power has given us everything we need for life and godliness through our knowledge of him who called us by his own
glory and goodness" (2 Peter 1:3).

THE PLAN OF THIS BOOK

This book is written for the average reader who recognizes
that anger is a too-frequent issue in his life and a too-prevalent
problem in his family, work, and church relationships. My own
experience certainly confirms this; the illustrations I'll share
from my own life and ministry verify the common place anger
has in our lives.

Further, this book provides pastors, counselors, and other
people-helpers with a practical Christ-centered resource to
guide them in their ministries and to pass on to those they serve.
Whether those ministries involve public preaching/teaching or

private discipling/counseling—the twofold ministry of the Word in Acts 20:20—this book aims to provide biblical counseling to help angry people change and grow. "Sanctify them by the truth; your word is truth" (John 17:17).

Chapter 1 presents an overview of biblical teaching on anger and defines anger as a whole-personed moral judgment against perceived evil. The next chapter offers practical criteria to distinguish righteous and sinful anger, illustrating the distinction with case studies of Bible characters.

The heart of the book—chapters 3 and 4—explores the roots of sinful anger and discovers its final cause to lie not in one's situation but in one's inner beliefs and motives. We then look at practical help to uproot our evil anger. The next pair of chapters presents some strategies for dealing with both revealed and concealed forms of angry behavior.

Chapter 7 addresses the problem of anger against God, while chapter 8 explores anger at yourself. I frequently encounter both in my counseling ministry. The former is more usual than we might admit and is often undefined; the latter is often misdiagnosed as the need to "forgive yourself."

Chapter 9 outlines a three-step ministry strategy that addresses the person's situation, heart, and behavior. While every reader can apply these to his own life, this chapter especially helps us to minister more wisely and compassionately to our friends and family members. First, we must develop a caring relationship and seek to understand both the person and his situation. Second, we must help him recognize and root out the cause of his sinful anger through changing his beliefs and motives. Third, we must help him control and correct his expression of sinful anger through changing his words and actions.

The final chapter seeks to motivate us to godly change based on God's warnings and promises. Readers will find that meditation on the three positive reasons, and the accompanying three negative ones, will aid their uprooting agenda. The appendices examine a pair of misunderstood "anger" texts, Ephesians 4:26 and Hebrews 12:15, and provide practical growth assignments to help you and others apply the book's truths.

Whether you tend to simmer or strike out, whether you implode or explode, there is biblical help for you. Jesus died and rose to help you uproot ungodly anger.

WHAT IS ANGER?

nger is a universal problem, prevalent in every culture, experienced by every generation. No one is isolated from its presence or immune from its poison. It permeates each person and spoils our most intimate relationships. Anger is a given part of our fallen human fabric.

Sadly, this is true even in our Christian homes and churches. The believer in Christ is not exempt from anger. His words and gestures betray it. He wrestles with its remnants within, realizing the task assigned by 1 Peter 2:11, "to abstain from sinful desires, which war against your soul," and heeding the call of Ephesians 4:31, to "get rid of all bitterness, rage and anger, brawling and slander, along with every form of malice." He battles it daily.

Jack became a Christian at age seventeen and met Jill when he was twenty-four. In their eleven years of marriage, God has blessed them with steady employment, a comfortable home, and two healthy children. In many ways, they are living the American middle-class dream. They are active members of their local church and serve Christ each week as Sunday-school teachers.

Yet beneath this veneer of success lurks long-standing relational dynamics of anger. A high achiever and hard worker, Jack drives himself and his family to perform up to his standards. And when he doesn't get the results he wants—Jill's affection, his supervisor's approval, his daughter's obedience—Jack explodes.

Jill, too, has an anger problem, though she rarely erupts. Inside she resents Jack for the demands he places on her and their daughters. At times she even feels betrayed by God. *Why did you let me marry him?* she murmurs to God. *I never knew it would turn out like this.* She resonates with that frustrated wife who once quipped, "When I married I was looking for a great deal, but instead found it to be an ordeal, and now I want a new deal."

Do you see the dynamic? Can you relate to it? Jill reacts to Jack's blowups by withdrawing; Jack reacts to her withdrawing by blowing up. They feed each other's anger, and, to extend the metaphor, they willingly digest it and reply in kind. Both attack and defend. Both retreat and wallow. Both feel justified. Meanwhile, their relational gulf widens, their children inhale their secondhand smoke, and God is dishonored. We'll return to Jack and Jill in a later chapter.

Anger is easier to describe than to define. We can't always dissect it, but we know it when we see it in others or feel it rising in our own veins. Our friend's protestation, "Angry? No, I'm not angry," rarely fools us, any more than our denials cover our angry expressions. You and I, and Jack and Jill, are more angry than we care to admit.

So what is anger? While the Bible presents no formal definition, it repeatedly pictures angry people. It uses a wide variety of terms that flavor our understanding. Scripture graphically describes the many forms of anger, warns us against sinful anger, and prescribes wise ways to uproot it.

A WORKING DEFINITION OF "ANGER"

Let's start with a working definition of "anger," a definition that brings together the biblical data into user-friendly categories.

OUR ANGER IS OUR WHOLE-PERSONED ACTIVE RESPONSE OF NEGATIVE MORAL JUDGMENT AGAINST PERCEIVED EVIL.

This definition imbeds several key ideas.

1. Our anger is an **active response**. It is an action, an activity. Anger is something we *do*, not something we *have*. It is not a thing, a fluid, or a force. The Bible pictures people who do anger, not have anger.

2. Our anger is a **whole-personed** active response. It involves our entire being and engages our whole person. We must resist various compartmentalized distinctions that emerge from pop psychology rather than from Scripture. Much popular literature labels anger as simply an "emotion."[1] Meanwhile, cognitive theorists stress belief systems, and behaviorists focus on angry reactions.

God's Word, of course, recognizes and addresses anger's many emotional, cognitive, volitional, and behavioral aspects. Anger in Scripture conveys emotion, spanning the spectrum from red-hot rage to icy-blue rejection. But it always involves beliefs and motives, perceptions and desires. And the Bible describes it in behavioral terms that are rich and graphic.

Yet the Bible does not slice the pie into neat analytic categories. Anger is more than mere emotion, volition, cognition, or behavior. Scripture resists simplistic schemes. Anger is complex. It comprises the whole person and encompasses our whole package of beliefs, feelings, actions, and desires.

3. Our anger is a **response against** something. It does not arise in a vacuum or appear spontaneously. Anger reacts against some provocation. Such a provocation, of course, must not be viewed as a causation ("He *made* me angry." "I was angry *because* my car broke down."). As we'll see in

15

chapter 3, anger's causal core lies in our active hearts. But our active hearts are always responding to the people and events in daily life.

4. Our anger, in essence, involves a **negative moral judgment** that we make. It arises from our judicial sense and functions under the larger dynamic of judgmentalism. In this sense, we may call anger a *"moral* emotion."[2] Anger protests, "What you did was *wrong!*" It pronounces, "That action is *unjust!*" It pleads, "This *must* stop!" Anger objects to wrongs committed.

We call it a "negative" moral judgment not because it is always sinful but because it *opposes* the perceived evil. Our anger postures us against what we determine to be evil. It casts negative mental votes against unjust actions. It determines that all offenders must change, be punished, or be removed. It issues mental death-penalty verdicts against the guilty. No wonder Jesus taught that anger is the moral equivalent of murder: "You have heard that it was said to the people long ago, 'Do not murder, and anyone who murders will be subject to judgment.' But I tell you that anyone who is angry with his brother will be subject to judgment" (Matt. 5:21–22). The apostle John repeats this truth: "Anyone who hates his brother is a murderer, and you know that no murderer has eternal life in him" (1 John 3:15).

There is, however, another sense in which our anger is moral. We do it before God's face, *coram Deo*, in the sight of him who gazes into the very depths of our being.[3] His eyes pierce and penetrate our inward beliefs and motives. And the God who sees most assuredly judges every aspect of our anger activity (Prov. 5:21; 15:3; 16:2; Jer. 17:9–10; Heb. 4:12–13).

5. Our anger involves a judgment against **perceived** evil. Our moral judgment arises from our personal perception. In anger we perceive some action, object, situation, or person to be evil or unjust. Jack and Jill see things in each other that they dislike and oppose.

Our perceptions, of course, may be accurate or inaccurate. We may assess the other person's actions in correct or incorrect ways. To further complicate things, our responses to our perceptions may then be godly or ungodly. In any event, our anger arises from our value system. It expresses our beliefs and motives. When a tyrant murders an innocent citizen, we perceive that act to be unjust and we react with anger. When the state executes a ruthless serial killer whose evil is beyond a reasonable doubt, we react with approval.

One theologian summarizes the biblical evidence for anger as judgmentalism: "Human anger is usually directed against other men. The reason for human anger can be that someone has been treated unjustly . . . , that one sees how other men are exploited . . . , or that one's fellow men manifest disobedience or unbelief in God."[4]

One benefit of our working definition is that it allows us to cut through some common smokescreens we might offer. "I'm not angry," we lamely protest. "I'm just frustrated (or bothered or upset)." But what the two different words might connote becomes irrelevant when we see that they both are reactions to some perceived unfairness or injustice. We may quibble about nuanced distinctions between such words as "anger" and "frustration," but the bottom line is that I am reacting to what you wrongly did to me.

Our working definition of "anger" lines up with the descriptions of several wise thinkers. The Puritan pastor Richard Baxter described anger as "the rising up in the heart in passionate displacency against an apprehended evil, which would cross or hinder us of some desired good."[5] Notice several key components in Baxter's definition. Anger comes from within, from "the heart." It includes a negative emotional response, a "passionate displacency." Anger opposes evil as we perceive it, "an apprehended evil." And we regard that person or situation as

17

evil because it interferes with what we want. It "would cross or hinder us of some desired good." Anger comes when circumstances or people thwart our lusts.

Another contemporary pastor offers a comparable definition: anger is "a hot displeasure of the heart or soul which is experienced in response to something you perceive to be wrong, and which calls for just retribution or repayment."[6] Again, anger includes the emotional experience of "hot displeasure." It arises from a fundamental perception of something as wrong. And it invites a volitional desire to repay.

BIBLICAL CATEGORIES OF ANGER

How does our definition fit the various forms of anger in Scripture? We can classify anger biblically into three categories: *divine anger, human righteous anger*, and *human sinful anger*.

Let's begin with *divine anger*, a subject that surprises many novice Bible readers. Statistically the vast majority of biblical references to anger are about God. One prominent Bible scholar observes that twenty different Hebrew words alone refer to God's indignation against evil.[7] All fourteen occurrences of the most frequent Hebrew verb (*anaph*) and 181 of the 229 occurrences of the related noun (*aph*) refer to God's anger. When we add the rest of the Old and New Testament vocabulary, we discover several hundred references to God's anger in the Bible. In one sense, God is both the most loving and the most angry person on our planet.

What does God's anger look like? Here our definition serves us well. God's anger is a whole-personed response involving his mind, will, affections, and actions. For example, the Hebrew terms mentioned above are sometimes translated as "nose," "nostrils," and "face" in reference to God's wrathful responses. These biblical anthropomorphisms—descriptions of God cast

18

in human forms—add color and heat to our understanding of God's anger. Consider these texts that tie anger to emotion:

> By the blast of your nostrils the waters piled up. The surging waters stood firm like a wall; the deep waters congealed in the heart of the sea. (Ex. 15:8)

> At the breath of God they are destroyed; at the blast of his anger they perish. (Job 4:9)

> The earth trembled and quaked, and the foundations of the mountains shook; they trembled because he was angry. Smoke rose from his nostrils; consuming fire came from his mouth, burning coals blazed out of it. . . . The valleys of the sea were exposed and the foundations of the earth laid bare at your rebuke, O Lord, at the blast of breath from your nostrils. (Ps. 18:7–8, 15)

Anger in Scripture—God's or ours—regularly radiates emotion. Anger is "hot"; it often "burns."

Against what, or whom, does God get angry? Using our definition, God's anger is his whole-personed active response of negative moral judgment against perceived evil. Simply put, God is angry with sinners and their sin. He maintains righteous wrath against all forms of wickedness. God's anger is his perfect, pure, settled opposition to evil. It is his holy abhorrence to everything that violates his character or misses his will. Surely one stands in awe of such graphic depictions as these:

> When I sharpen my flashing sword and my hand grasps it in judgment, I will take vengeance on my adversaries and repay those who hate me. (Deut. 32:41)

> The One enthroned in heaven laughs; the Lord scoffs at them. Then he rebukes them in his anger and terrifies them in his wrath. . . . (Ps. 2:4–5)

19

God is a righteous judge, a God who expresses his wrath every day. (Ps. 7:11)

Nor does the New Testament present a kinder, gentler God:

Whoever believes in the Son has eternal life, but whoever rejects the Son will not see life, for God's wrath remains on him. (John 3:36)

The wrath of God is being revealed from heaven against all the godlessness and wickedness of men who suppress the truth by their wickedness. . . . (Rom. 1:18; cf. 2:5–9, 16)

Furthermore, God's anger flows from his justice. It arises from God's negative moral judgment against perceived evil, and unlike us, he always perceives evil with utter accuracy.

For example, Numbers 25:11 hails Phinehas as the one who "turned [God's] anger away" from Israel by his bold act of spearing an immoral couple. God's righteous wrath had abided on his people because of their sin. God's anger reflects his accurate perception of evil, his holy hatred of it, and his determination to eradicate it; or, here, to accept atonement for it (cf. Rom. 3:21–26).

Second, Scripture speaks of *righteous human anger*. Here we can include Jesus' anger, although as the God-Man he bridges both categories. We see this, for example, in Psalm 2:12's description of the messianic Son: "Kiss the Son, lest he be angry and you be destroyed in your way, for his wrath can flare up in a moment. Blessed are all who take refuge in him." We see the connection here between anger and divine judgment. The Messiah's fury arises against wicked rebels and brings them punishment.

Righteous human anger imitates God's anger. It is our negative response to the evil that we accurately perceive as being evil. In Exodus 32:19–20, Moses reproduced the same burning anger against the Israelites that God had revealed against them earlier (32:9–10) and would reveal against them later in the same chapter (32:33–35). We will explore our Lord Jesus' anger and some additional exhibitions of righteous human anger in our next chapter.

A third category of anger—the focus of this book—is *sinful human anger*. As a biblical survey would suggest, nearly all human anger is sinful.[8] Passages such as James 1:13–15 and 3:13–4:12 unpack the subtleties of our evil, deceitful desires. An honest assessment of our life and ministry verifies how rarely human anger is righteous.

Do you remember our definition? Anger is our whole-personed active response of negative moral judgment against perceived evil. This approach helps us pinpoint the specific ways in which our anger might be sinful.

For example, in some cases our perceptions are wrong. We are blind to what is truly sinful. Deceitful lies or self-centered lusts rule us. Perhaps ignorance or impulsiveness twists our perspectives. Our judgments are askew. We impugn other people's motives. In other cases, our responses are ungodly. They violate God's will in their form, their degree, or their timing. We will examine these insights in chapter 3 and subsequent chapters.

TOURING THE BIBLE'S PICTURE GALLERY

Let's walk down the hallway of our Bible and peek into some angry rooms to see how the Bible's characters demonstrate our definition. We'll see how the common thread of judgmentalism drives every case.

In the first recorded case of anger, Cain was mad at God because he assumed that God was unjust (Gen. 4:5). He *wanted* God to accept his sacrifice on his terms, and he *believed* God should do so. Anger always starts in the heart, with evil desires and wrong beliefs—lusts and lies.

The Old Testament patriarchs provide plenty of examples. Esau's anger with deceitful Jacob in Genesis 27 follows the pattern we have already seen. Having discovered his brother's double treachery of stealing his birthright and now his blessing, Esau held a grudge and plotted his murder. Rightly did Rebekah describe him as furious and angry.

Sometimes anger ignites pointed words. Jealous of Leah's fruitfulness, Rachel pleaded desperately with Jacob for children in Genesis 30:1–2. Jacob responded angrily to her nagging with a sharp rebuke: "Am I in the place of God, who has kept you from having children?"

More often in Scripture, anger brings violent outbursts or punitive actions, as in Potiphar's anger against Joseph in Genesis 39. Having perceived—albeit inaccurately—Joseph's wrongdoing, he erupted with hot anger and proceeded to imprison him. Ironically, in Genesis 44, Judah implored this same Joseph—whose identity was yet unknown to Judah—not to be angry with him and his brothers. Judah rightly feared this now-exalted Joseph's power to imprison, enslave, or kill them for their apparently unlawful conduct.

Or consider Moses. Provoked by the people's rapid, idolatrous declension, "his anger burned and he threw the tablets out of his hands" (Ex. 32:19). Similar language marks Jacob (Gen. 30:2; 31:36), Balaam (Num. 22:27), Balak (Num. 24:10), Saul (1 Sam. 18:8; 20:30), David (2 Sam. 6:8; 12:5), Jonah (Jonah 4:1), and others. In each case, the angry person perceives someone as wrong and reacts with various negative feelings and behavior.

In 2 Chronicles 25:5–13 King Amaziah of Judah unwisely hired one hundred thousand Israelite soldiers, and then at God's directive dismissed them before they saw military action. The troops responded with great rage to this perceived mistreatment—an inaccurate perception because it was God who was behind their dismissal. Like a pink-slipped employee "going postal" or taking revenge on the boss's kids, they raided many Judean towns and killed three thousand occupants. Similarly, Elihu reacted in anger against Job for his apparent self-justification and against Job's friends for condemning but not refuting Job (Job 32:1–5). Elihu in turn addressed them all with passionate reproofs.

Tracing another frequent Hebrew term *(hemah)* through the book of Esther is especially instructive, since judging—sometimes righteous, sometimes unrighteous—underlies each occurrence. King Xerxes raged when his independent queen, Vashti, ignored his summons to attend the feast (Est. 1:12; 2:1). He regarded her actions as a personal insult. Next, his evil official Haman "burned" against Mordecai the Jew and plotted his destruction (3:5; 5:9). Finally, with classic irony, Haman the judge becomes judged himself. The king rages against Haman and executes him on the same gallows that Haman had built for Mordecai (7:7, 10). Haman's life is a tragic testimony to the truth that violent men "lie in wait for their own blood; they waylay only themselves!" (Prov. 1:18).

Stemming from a Semitic root for a storm or violent rain, another Hebrew term *(za'aph)* often carries the idea of rage or aroused anger. With pathetic irony, the wisdom writer observed that "a man's own folly ruins his life, yet his heart rages against the LORD" (Prov. 19:3), while 2 Chronicles describes the sinful wrath of Asa (2 Chron. 16:10) and Uzziah (26:19), and the righteous wrath of God (28:9). Each of these angry individuals responded to perceived evil or unfairness.

Besides these Hebrew terms, the book of Daniel uses a pair of Aramaic terms for "anger" that both convey judgmentalism. King Nebuchadnezzar is angry with his so-called wise men for their inability to interpret his dream (Dan. 2:12). He later reacts with fury against the three Hebrew young men who refuse to worship the idolatrous image he raised (3:13, 19).

What do we find in all these Old Testament texts? Angry people respond with their whole being—their thoughts, emotions, affections, words, actions, etc.—to people they perceive to be wrong or harmful to their own interests. Those reactions are frequently hot reactions. Often—always with God and sometimes with humans—that perception and the accompanying response are just and warranted. In other cases—never with God and usually with humans—they are not. The resulting anger is sinful.

We find the same realities in the New Testament. The three word groups for "anger" largely reflect divine anger or human sinful anger, with little allowance for righteous anger.[9] While many appear as commands or prohibitions (e.g., Gal. 5:20; Eph. 4:31; Col. 3:8; 1 Tim. 2:8; James 1:19–20), a number of narrative passages picture angry people.

Driven to eliminate all competition, King Herod became enraged in his pursuit of the baby born to be a king (Matt. 2:16). Synagogue worshipers turned against Jesus angrily and tried to kill him after he had reminded them that God's grace extends to Gentiles and not just Jews (Luke 4:28), while a synagogue ruler became indignant with Jesus when Jesus violated his sense of religious propriety by healing a crippled woman on the Sabbath (Luke 13:14). Jewish leaders responded similarly when they saw Jesus healing people and heard children shouting, "Hosanna to the Son of David" (Matt. 21:15). Christ's disciples expressed anger at James and John's request for special seating status in his kingdom (Matt. 20:24; Mark 10:41).

The gospels and Acts provide further examples of real life people reacting with anger based on their negative moral judgments against perceived evil.

To complete our general understanding of anger, let's assess some popular efforts to classify anger into three distinct categories based on the three New Testament word groups for "anger." Some Christian psychologists, in their attempt to "integrate" the Bible with their particular psychological approach, posit a tripartite scheme of rage, resentment, and indignation, based particularly on the supposed distinctions between the Greek words.[10] Helping people understand their type or form of anger is part of these psychologists' treatment plan.

How shall we evaluate this threefold categorization? While many careful New Testament scholars admit that "a slight shift of emphasis" can sometimes be seen between these word groups,[11] they conclude that there is "no material difference between them"[12] and that they are largely synonymous, even appearing in the same passages without distinction (Eph. 4:31; Col. 3:8). Whatever occasional nuanced differences may exist between these word groups, there is little justification for this kind of neat classification structure. The Bible resists such reductionism. The width of the spectrum of human anger—yours and mine—defies simple categories.

All of the Bible's anger words, however, in the Old and New Testament accounts, do clearly show us real people who form negative moral judgments in the face of the evil they see and who respond to that perceived wrongness in whole-personed ways—in their desires, thoughts, emotions, words, actions, and goals.

Whether our moral judgments and resulting reactions are right or wrong, godly or evil, and how to tell the difference, will be the subject of our next chapter.

For Further Reflection and Life Application

1. Look up in a concordance the places where the words "anger" (and "angry," "angered"), "wrath," and

"rage" appear in the Bible. Read through them and notice how many references pertain to God's anger. And notice the range of people and range of behavior associated with anger in the Bible.

2. Reflect on Richard Baxter's description of anger on page 17 above. Where in your life do you see his words defining you? Pay particular attention to those times when something or someone "would cross or hinder [you] of some desired good."

3. Jot down a typical anger episode in your life. Note the situation in which your anger arose, any provoking or triggering factors, what you wanted but were not getting (or didn't want but were getting), and what your anger actually looked like.

IS YOUR ANGER REALLY RIGHTEOUS?

Sure, I was angry," declared Clarence, "but I had a right to be angry." His reluctant admission was quickly followed by a rhetorical question, one that many pastors have heard too many times: "After all, didn't Jesus Christ get angry?"

Clarence's comments came after another intense blowup at his wife, Judy, and their hard-to-handle teenager. The domestic rage had escalated until Judy issued the ultimatum, "Get help, or get out!" Filled with fear, embarrassment, and frustration, Clarence made the right choice and came to his pastor for help.

Clarence's case is not uncommon. "Sure, I was angry, but it was righteous anger." How often have you heard that? How often have you *said* that? And what do we make of Clarence's words? Was he correct? Was his anger Christlike? How do you assess whether your anger, or your friend's anger, is righteous anger or sinful anger? The Bible pictures both. How do we know?

THE DANGER OF SELF-DECEPTION

Let's begin with a humbling observation: most human anger is sinful. The biblical record confirms this. The most frequent Old Testament term for "anger" (Hebrew *aph*) denotes human anger forty-seven times. And at least forty-two of them—eighty-nine percent—indicate sinful anger.

While we tend to assume the best about ourselves, the Bible frequently warns against self-deception. We tend to conceal our sins, covering them with spiritual whiteout. We paint our anger as pure. The Bible knows better:

The heart is deceitful above all things and beyond cure. . . . (Jer. 17:9)

Put off your old self, which is being corrupted by its deceitful desires. . . . (Eph. 4:22)

See to it, brothers, that none of you has a sinful, unbelieving heart that turns away from the living God. But encourage one another daily, as long as it is called Today, so that none of you may be hardened by sin's deceitfulness. (Heb. 3:12–13)

This simple warning ought to color any consideration of the "righteousness" of our anger. We must approach this question with a keen awareness of this danger.

The prophet Jonah provides a classic case of self-deception. Jonah 4 records that "Jonah was greatly displeased and became angry." Twice God confronts him with same question: "Have you any right to be angry?" Jonah's reply? "I do," he said. "I am angry enough to die." God's self-deceived prophet asserts the legitimacy of his rage. God's reply and the flow of the narrative make it plain that Jonah was wrong. For Jonah, anger was not a God-given right. Jonah had no justification for justifying his sinful anger as righteous.

Given the danger of self-deception, how can we distinguish sinful anger from righteous anger? How can we discern whether our anger is indeed Christlike, and help the Clarences (and Claras) in our world? More importantly, how can we do so based on *biblical* criteria?

THREE CRITERIA OF RIGHTEOUS ANGER

Let's consider three distinguishing marks—three differential criteria—of righteous anger, and then observe these criteria in Jesus and several other biblical characters. Our goal is to encourage righteous anger and expose its frequent counterfeits.

1. Righteous Anger Reacts against Actual Sin

Righteous anger arises from an accurate perception of true evil, from sin as defined biblically, i.e., as a violation of God's Word (Rom. 3:23; 1 John 3:4), any "want of conformity unto, or transgression of, the law of God."[1] Righteous anger does not result from merely being inconvenienced or from violations of personal preference or human tradition. It responds to sin as objectively defined by God's Word, including violations of both of our Lord's great commandments (Matt. 22:36–40).

2. Righteous Anger Focuses on God and His Kingdom, Rights, and Concerns, Not on Me and My Kingdom, Rights, and Concerns

In Scripture, God-centered motives, not self-centered motives, drive righteous anger. Righteous anger focuses on how people offend God and his name, not me and my name. It terminates on God more than me. In other words, accurately viewing something as offensive is not enough. We must view it primarily as offending God.

Righteous anger throbs with kingdom concerns.

3. Righteous Anger Is Accompanied by Other Godly Qualities and Expresses Itself in Godly Ways

Righteous anger remains self-controlled. It keeps its head without cursing, screaming, raging, or flying off the handle. Nor does it spiral downward in self-pity or despair. It does not ignore people, snub people, or withdraw from people. Instead, righteous anger carries with it the twin qualities of confidence

29

and self-control. Christlike anger is not all-consuming and myopic but channeled to sober, earnest ends. Godly strains of mourning, comfort, joy, praise, and action balance it.

Rather than keeping us from carrying out God's call, righteous anger leads to godly expressions of worship, ministry, and obedience. It shows concern for the well-being of others. It rises in defense of oppressed people. It seeks justice for victims. It rebukes transgressors. Godly anger confronts evil and calls for repentance and restoration.

David Powlison asks seven questions to help someone assess whether his or her anger is righteous:[2] (1) Do you get angry about the right things? (2) Do you express your anger in the right way? (3) How long does your anger last? (4) How controlled is your anger? (5) What motivates your anger? (6) Is your anger "primed and ready" to respond to another person's habitual sins? (7) What is the effect of your anger?

Notice how these questions wisely reflect our three criteria: Question 1 points us to our first criterion, anger against actual sin. Questions 5 and 6 address our second criterion, anger that is God-centered. And questions 2, 3, 4, and 7 explore various aspects of our third criterion, anger expressed in godly ways and accompanied by godly fruit.

OUR LORD'S RIGHTEOUS ANGER

If Clarence's frequent bouts of anger are indeed "righteous like Christ's," then we need to examine Jesus' anger. What do we see when we study the Scriptures? Prophetically, the psalms picture the coming Christ as a King whose "wrath can flare up in a moment" and who has "love[d] righteousness and hate[d] wickedness" (Ps. 2:12; 45:7; cf. Heb. 1:9). Other Old Testament passages picture the Messiah as the coming Judge who will rescue and restore his people and punish his enemies with awful vengeance.

In turning to the gospels, one might expect to find a host of anger displays in Jesus. Ready for a surprise? Despite popular notions, in only a few cases do we see an angry Savior. Judging from the Bible's record, anger was uncommon for Jesus, and certainly far less than we see it in Clarence and ourselves. Chronic anger simply does not characterize his life. Despite daily provocations from others, his anger was limited to specific occasions.

Let's consider the three clear, specific occasions in light of our criteria. While there may be additional exhibits,[3] we will limit our study to the three occasions when the Bible uses explicit anger language to describe Jesus.

Exhibit 1: Jesus and the Pharisees (Mark 3:1–6)

In Mark 3:1–6, Jesus meets a man on a Sabbath day in need of healing. Because of their wrong notions of the Sabbath, the Pharisees oppose our Lord's intention to heal him. How did our Lord respond? "He looked around at them in anger and, deeply distressed at their stubborn hearts, said to the man, 'Stretch out your hand.' He stretched it out, and his hand was completely restored" (v. 5).

Consider our criteria for righteous anger. Jesus accurately perceived the Pharisees' sin—their hard hearts displayed in their critical eye toward him, their refusal to answer his piercing question, and their murderous plot. Moreover, they lacked mercy and compassion for the suffering man. Clearly, Christ's anger is a reaction against their actual sin (criterion #1).

Yet this reaction was more than a response to a personal offense. The Pharisees' sin opposed and hindered Jesus' *mission* as God's appointed Messiah. In the flow of Mark's narrative, Jesus' healing ministry attested to his messianic call (2:12), and his deliberate choice of the Sabbath day underscored his lordship over it (2:27–28). To despise and oppose Jesus' healing work is to despise and oppose the advancement

31

of God's redemptive plan, to interrupt his messianic program and prolong the rule of Satan. Our Lord's anger was closely connected to God and his kingdom, rights, and concerns (criterion #2).

How did Jesus' anger show itself? With perfect self-control. He kept his head, not venting rage or flying off the handle. Nor did this righteous anger immobilize him or prevent his healing work. He remained sober and bold in ministering to the crippled man. Our Lord did not put his God-given task on hold while he went to "cool off." He didn't suspend his ministry to this needy person until finishing with his pharisaical critics. He pressed on despite their furious opposition and plots to kill him. Fearing God, he feared no one else. He courageously pursued justice and mercy as he carried out his Father's mission (criterion #3).

Exhibit 2: Jesus and His Disciples (Mark 10:13–16)

In Mark 10 we again see Jesus angry, yet not against his enemies but against his own disciples. A group of people brought their children for Jesus to touch and bless them, yet for reasons unstated his disciples rebuked these parents. In the face of such cold mistreatment *against others*, our Lord became indignant with the disciples. Whatever their motives, these disciples effectively prevented these little ones (and perhaps their parents) from knowing him (criterion #1).

What fueled our Lord's anger? An unyielding desire for the extension of God's kingdom drove him: "do not hinder them, for the kingdom of God belongs to such as these" (v. 15). The disciples hindered that righteous desire. Passion for God's kingdom consumed Christ, not his own popularity, fame, approval, or "need" to feel needed (criterion #2).

While our Lord earnestly wanted these specific children to enter the kingdom, a careful reading suggests a broader passion. Jesus seized their approach as an opportunity to illustrate the nature of saving faith. The kingdom, he contended, does not belong to children per se (i.e., young humans more than older humans). It belongs to those "such as these" (v. 14), those who will "receive the kingdom of God like a little child" (v. 15). The childlike receptivity pictures helplessness. Our Lord was using a visual illustration that the kingdom is "received" by helpless people, by grace through faith (Luke 12:32; Heb. 12:28). His anger arose because his disciples spoiled this powerful illustration of salvation by grace through faith. They hindered God's gospel and undercut his kingdom.

How did Jesus behave in the midst of his righteous anger? As in Mark 3, he manifested self-control. He did not fly into a rage. Nor did his anger deter his ministry. He loved these children, held them, and blessed them (v. 16). He did not call a "timeout" to reprimand his disciples. He rebuked his disciples, then focused his attention on the children and pursued his Father's will to bless them (criterion #3).

Exhibit 3: Jesus and the Temple Merchants (John 2:13–17)

John 2 records one of perhaps two occasions when Jesus cleansed the temple of those who were making it into a marketplace.[4] Merchants were selling animals—presumably for temple sacrifices—and exchanging money in the Jerusalem temple courts to facilitate those sales. Matthew's parallel account explicitly declares their unlawfulness: " 'It is written,' he said to them, ' "My house will be called a house of prayer," but you are making it a "den of robbers" ' " (Matt 21:13, quoting Isa. 56:7 and Jer. 7:11). Such activities dishonored God's temple and victimized the poor. Again, our Lord reacts against actual sin (criterion #1).

Why do we view this passage as an anger passage? While neither John nor the other gospel writers use anger words for what Jesus did, one such word does appear in verse 17: "His disciples remembered that it is written: 'Zeal for your house

33

will consume me.' " The term "zeal" carries the flavor of anger and indignation. Hebrews 10:27 couples it with God's wrath, the "raging fire that will consume the enemies of God." One writer defines our Lord's zeal here as his "hot indignation at the pollution of the house of God,"[5] while another calls it "burning jealousy for the holiness of the house of God."[6]

Zeal, yes. But zeal for whose house? What drove Jesus' anger? It was zeal for God's house, not personal revenge. They were not polluting and defiling *his* house, but *his Father's* house. For Jesus, it was not "about me" but "about my Father" (criterion #2).

What marked Jesus' anger? What accompanied and arose from it (criterion #3)? Again we see our Lord remaining under control. While sinful anger screams, curses, vents, and rages, righteous anger maintains a godly demeanor. Yet our Lord's controlled anger was not weak. It was confrontational. Fortified with power, his anger showed itself in bold judicial acts. Christ focused his energy to bring judgment against evil. He drove out the animals with a whip. He scattered the coins, overturned the tables, and commanded the dove-sellers to vacate the premises immediately.

In this judicial act, motivated by God's glory, we see a foretaste of Christ's final displays of judgment. Revelation 6:16–17 pictures one such scene: "They called to the mountains and the rocks, 'Fall on us and hide us from the face of him who sits on the throne and from the wrath of the Lamb! For the great day of their wrath has come, and who can stand?' "

In summary, Christ's anger displayed three criteria to assess the righteousness or unrighteousness of our own anger. It reacted against actual sin (criterion #1). It focused on God and his kingdom, rights, and concerns more than his own. And it arose not because people had sinned against him but because they had sinned against his Father and against other people (criterion #2). Furthermore, other godly qualities and expressions accompanied it. Jesus was not cold, stoic, and uncaring about God's honor and other people's welfare. Nor did he throw fits or withdraw. He ministered to people (criterion #3).

But what about sinful offenses aimed at him personally? How did Jesus respond? Amazingly, not with anger! Instead, 1 Peter 2:21–23 describes his reaction to severe abuse. Jesus entrusted himself and his enemies to God his Father, the righteous Judge (v. 23; cf. 4:19; Rom. 12:19). He did not take revenge or sin with his tongue (vv. 22–23). Instead, he did good (4:19) by praying for his enemies' forgiveness (Luke 23:34a). Having laid down his personal "rights" (Phil. 2:5–11), he was free to serve his enemies without anger.

RIGHTEOUS ANGER IN SAUL AND JONATHAN

Our Lord is not the only example of righteous human anger. Even fallen sinners can display godly anger. Consider three cases.[7]

In 1 Samuel 11:1–6, Nahash the Ammonite attacked the Israelite city of Jabesh Gilead. The residents cowered in fear and offered their surrender. Saul heard about the episode and, as verse 6 records, the Holy Spirit came powerfully on him and produced burning anger.

This Spirit-produced anger meets our three criteria: It responded to the Ammonite's sinful military arrogance before God and violent subjugation of others. It focused not on Saul's good per se but on the good of God and his covenant people. And it led to clearheaded, bold obedience. Saul did not sit and stew all day. He did not fly off the handle or retreat in shame. Like Jesus cleansing the temple, Saul rose to the occasion and pressed the military campaign with Spirit-given anger.

First Samuel 20:24–35 unveils a moving Old Testament account of righteous anger. Saul—no longer Spirit-filled—

35

schemed to eliminate David, his royal competitor and the God-appointed successor to the throne. With his kingdom threatened and his self-centered idols undercut, Saul erupted in sinful rage. He hurled a spear at his son Jonathan because Jonathan had (rightly) sided with David against his father, Saul.

How would we assess Jonathan's anger? Clearly, he reacted in anger to Saul's sin (criterion #1). Yet against which sin? Was it Saul's sin of hurling a spear at Jonathan or Saul's sin of hating and plotting the murder of God's king, David? The answer is startling: Jonathan was more angry with Saul for seeking to kill King David than for seeking to kill him (criterion #2)! Saul's drive to kill God's anointed king upset Jonathan more than Saul's throwing the spear. In addition, this anger led Jonathan to take wise and bold action—to rendezvous with David and inform him of Saul's mission (criterion #3).

Believers hail Psalm 119 as a tribute to God's Word, a symphony exalting Scripture. Yet it is more than that. It testifies to the inspired writer's total devotion to knowing and obeying that Word. Notice how our three criteria repeatedly emerge in the following passages, along with a wide gamut of godly emotional responses.

In verses 52–54, the psalmist experiences "indignation" toward ungodly people. It grips him; he is in its clutches. Such righteous anger is no passing feeling, fleeting thought, or momentary emotion.

> I remember your ancient laws, O LORD, and I find comfort in them. Indignation grips me because of the wicked, who have forsaken your law. Your decrees are the theme of my song wherever I lodge.

His indignation does not come from personal annoyance but is a settled reaction against those who forsake God's law. Nor is it myopic. The text sandwiches righteous anger between comfort and praise. Righteous anger coexists with confidence and with joyful singing.

Several passages speak of the psalmist's hatred of "wrong paths," basing his judgment not on personal preferences but on God's Word:

> How sweet are your words to my taste, sweeter than honey to my mouth! I gain understanding from your precepts; therefore I hate every wrong path. (vv. 103–4)

> Because I love your commands more than gold, more than pure gold, and because I consider all your precepts right, I hate every wrong path. (vv. 127–28)

At the same time, this sense of hatred coexists, without contradiction, with a sense of sweet delight in God's Word. The psalmist is not a raging bull; he is a lover of God's truth and a hater of anything that opposes it.

Yet not only does the writer hate wrong paths, he also hates those who walk on them: "I hate double-minded men, but I love your law. You are my refuge and my shield; I have put my hope in your word. Away from me, you evildoers, that I may keep the commands of my God!" (vv. 113–15).

What drives his godly hatred? His love for God and his Word. Along with hatred he expresses disdain, a desire to distance himself from evildoers who hinder him from obeying God. His attitude simply reflects God's antipathy for the wicked.

Few sections of Scripture present the range of godly emotion better than Psalm 119. In verses 135–36, we witness not his anger, as in previous verses, but his godly mourning. Streams of tears flow from the believer's eyes: "Make your face shine upon your servant and teach me your decrees. Streams of tears flow from my eyes, for your law is not obeyed" (vv. 135–36).

37

What has broken this floodgate of tears? Not some personal hurt but the rejection by others of God and his truth. Such feelings arise from the psalmist's commitment to learn and follow God's Word. We feel the same emotional drain in verse 139: "My zeal wears me out, for my enemies ignore your words." His zeal, akin to Psalm 69:9 and John 2:17, so grips him that he is worn out. The Hebrew verb carries the idea of extermination. Why does he experience such pain? Because his enemies willfully ignore not his words but God's words.

Consider the common experience of being snubbed in a social setting. Recall times when someone failed to return your phone call promptly, if at all. Did you feel ignored? Were you tempted to respond with "righteous" anger? Remember that the psalmist's anger arose because people ignored God, not because they ignored him. He loathes, and pities, the ungodly not because they persecute him but because they oppose God:

> Many are the foes who persecute me, but I have not turned from your statutes. I look on the faithless with loathing, for they do not obey your word. See how I love your precepts; preserve my life, O LORD, according to your love. (vv. 157–59)

Although their persecution of him is the bad fruit of rejecting God, it is their disobedience against God more than their persecution of him that fuels his righteous anger. Self-retaliation, self-defense, and self-protection did not drive him. Setting "boundaries" was not his goal. He trusted the Lord as his protector. Love for God and his Word anchored him.

One last text completes our sweep of Psalm 119. In verses 162–64, the godly heart hates falsehood:

> I rejoice in your promise like one who finds great spoil. I hate and abhor falsehood but I love your law. Seven times a day I praise you for your righteous laws.

Yet this hatred and abhorrence are not all-consuming. They are coupled with great joy and praise in the psalmist's heart. Both his hatred and his rapture arise from the same root: love for Scripture and a conviction that it is righteous.

ASSESSING OUR OWN ANGER

Based on our study of Jesus and the Bible characters above, we conclude that three criteria mark righteous anger:

1. It reacts against actual sin (as biblically defined).
2. It focuses on God and his concerns (not me and my concerns).
3. It coexists with other godly qualities and expresses itself in godly ways.

Our study summons us to two major growth agendas and ministry concerns. First, we must expose our pseudo-righteous anger. This requires repenting not only of the anger itself, which we now discover to have been *sinful* anger, but also of our self-deceived justification of it in the name of "righteous" anger. The facade falls away when we carefully place our anger before the mirror of our three biblical criteria. Scripture exposes our anger as sinful. This invites fresh opportunities to repent and believe, to draw near to God, and to more accurately know Christ and ourselves.

Consider times when your spouse offends you. In the name of "righteous anger," do you ever rail against him or her? Do you ignore or withdraw from your mate? Do you spiral downward in self-pity? Do his or her offenses consume your mind? Do you cancel your plans for that evening or suspend your service for Christ that weekend? Or do you simply kick the dog, or the door? If so, your anger is not Christlike.

39

Suppose your son rebels. Perhaps he defies your curfew limit or speaks disrespectfully to you. Do you blow up in rage or retaliate with reckless words? Do you take it out on your spouse or others? Do you give up on your son or begin to avoid him? Do you daily replay the scene in your mind? Do you lose control or become obsessed over it? If so, your anger is not righteous.

Or what happens inside you when your boss bypasses you for a promotion, after you've worked hard to address the blind spots noted in your last evaluation? Does your disappointment turn to anger, and do you justify that anger with a growing edge in your voice? *That lousy supervisor doesn't know a good worker when he sees one. It must be because I'm a Christian that he treats me this way.* Do you walk the path of martyrdom, assuming your indignation to be righteous, the godly response against "persecution"?

While an offending spouse, rebellious teen, or unfair boss can tempt (not cause) an anger response, you must ask yourself some key questions: Are you angry because of what the person did to you, or what he or she did to your Savior? Whom do you regard as the one most offended—you or Jesus? In the midst of your heated emotion, are you consumed with yourself or with your God? Does your indignation arise because God's name is dishonored, or because your pride has been hurt? Righteous anger arises because of the other person's sin against God, not because of your personal hurts or vengeful desires.

St. Augustine of Hippo understood this. In his famous work *The Confessions*, the fourth-century church father comments on a time when he became angry. Prior to his conversion, he came to Rome at the age of twenty-nine to launch his career as a teacher of rhetoric. Upon his arrival, he began to gather students but soon became aware of a particular ploy that many of them used. "To avoid paying their teacher's salary, a number of youths would suddenly plot together and go to another teacher, breakers of faith, who for love of money hold justice cheap."[8]

How did Augustine respond? "My heart hated them, though not with a 'perfect hatred' (Ps. 139:22), for perhaps I hated them *more because I was to suffer by them than because they did things utterly unlawful*" (emphasis added).[9] In other words, Augustine's anger fell short of being righteous—it was not the perfect hatred of the psalmist. Why not? Because it terminated on himself and his financial loss more than on the righteous laws that the perpetrators had broken.

Later, however, after his conversion and growth as a Christian, Augustine looked back on these offenders with a more righteous anger. "And now I hate such depraved and crooked people, though I love them if they are set right so that instead of money they prefer the learning which they acquire and learning of You, O God, the truth and fullness of assured goodness and peace."[10] What changed? His consciousness of God. Augustine's anger toward the offenders became oriented toward their rejection of God. Yet like the psalmist above, concurrent with his hatred we hear a desire that they would come to know and love God more than money. "But at that time," Augustine concludes, "I would rather, *for my own sake*, have disliked them for being evil than to have liked and wished them good for You" (emphasis added).[11]

Let's return to Clarence, the dad who defended his so-called righteous anger. "Sure, I was angry," declared Clarence, "but I had a right to be angry."

The Lord used our three criteria to convict Clarence of his pseudo-righteous anger. His claims of "righteous anger" in response to his teenager's disobedience merely covered his own ungoverned wrath. How so? He had viewed his daughter as existing to make his world convenient and orderly. But she did not fit his tidy agenda. When she failed to live by her dad's script, he became angry. The fact that she was also failing to live by God's Word was of only marginal importance to Clarence at the time.

Clarence confessed his anger and its pretended "righteousness." While his daughter's disobedience and back talk were sinful (thus satisfying criterion #1), this fact merely helped him rationalize his wrong response. Thoughts of God's injured honor were—by his own later admission—the furthest thing from his mind when he exploded (thus missing criterion #2). Moreover, he was anything but Christlike in how he responded to his daughter (violating criterion #3). Her well-being was not on his radar screen. "It was all about me, not her," he later confessed.

Once Clarence repented of his sinful anger and his self-deception, he could minister more effectively to his daughter. And his wife became more supportive. In fact, that ministry began the day he humbly asked them both to forgive him, not only for his outbursts but also for rationalizing them.

A second godly agenda and ministry concern flows from our study: we must not only expose our pseudo-righteous anger, but also cultivate righteous anger. If God is angry over sin, then growth in godliness entails a corresponding growth in righteous anger.

Although no single text commands us to be angry,[12] both the passages discussed above and the holy character of God revealed throughout Scripture form a solid call to righteous anger. Christlikeness includes Christlike anger. The absence of righteous anger when it is appropriate is as sinful as the presence of sinful anger.

I write this chapter as an American pastor and seminary professor several years after the tragic events of September 11, 2001. On that dreadful day, terrorists skyjacked jet planes and crashed them into New York City's World Trade Center and Washington's Pentagon, killing more than three thousand people. The rage of my fellow Americans to this day remains hot. But the motives behind that rage—according to the biblical criteria exemplified in Jesus and the other Bible characters mentioned above—are surely mixed.

How can you cultivate godly anger? Double back through the many texts cited in this chapter and ask God by his Spirit to reproduce this godly trait in you.

What does cultivating godly anger involve? Refocus your heart on God and his kingdom, rights, and concerns. Repent of your self-centered desires. Meditate on God's actions and attributes. Passion for God is the sole seedbed for righteous anger. It alone produces hatred of sin. A deepening love for God and his Word and ways creates a corresponding loathing of those who harden themselves against him. To delight in truth is to disdain evil. Rejoicing in righteousness makes wickedness repulsive.

Clarence has begun to take steps in this progress. He has asked God to fill him with a holy hatred about his own anger, to realize how quickly he ascends the throne and plays God whenever his daughter or his wife disappoints him. He is also asking God to help him hate not his daughter but her remaining sin that deceives and seeks to enslave her.

While no single text *commands* righteous anger, Hebrews 1:9, quoting messianically from Psalm 45:7 about our Lord Jesus, holds before us his perfect example:

> You have loved righteousness and hated wickedness;
> therefore God, your God, has set you above your
>   companions
> by anointing you with the oil of joy.

For Further Reflection and Life Application

1. At the very next moment you are tempted to view some angry response within yourself as "righteous," stop! Remind yourself of the dangers of self-deception and review the three criteria above, along with some of the Bible passages we considered. Test your anger against this biblical standard. And do so ruthlessly. Take no captives.

2. There are at least two more practical steps that will help you. First, write down why you are angry and your seeming rationale for labeling your anger as righteous. Second, invite a pastor, elder, or mature Christian friend to help you assess your claim.

3. Read Psalm 119 at one or two sittings, paying attention not only to the psalmist's devotion to God's Word (the usual way we look at Psalm 119), but also to the wide range of godly emotions he experiences and varied responses he exhibits.

4. Memorize Hebrews 1:9a, "You have loved righteousness and hated wickedness," and ask God to fill you with this dual spirit of Christ. Interview two or three mature Christian friends to learn what righteous anger might look like in their lives and how they cultivate it.

GETTING TO THE HEART OF ANGER

3

Like you and me, Jack and Jill have an anger problem. Jack blows; Jill clams. He rants and raves; she simmers and stews.

It's Thursday. Jack returns at 6:30 from a pressured workday eager to enjoy a tasty meal and a relaxing evening with his family. Unfortunately, the house is cluttered and the kids are wild. Supper isn't ready; it is not even started. "All I want is to come home to a peaceful house," he yells to Jill. "Is that too much to ask? This place is a mess!" He then compounds the problem by asking that proverbially provocative question that no right-minded spouse should ever ask: "Just what have you been doing all day around here?"

Jill is also angry, but she doesn't yell back, at least this time. Her anger is more icy-blue than red-hot. Jill resents Jack's criticism, his yelling, and his lack of tenderness. In turn, she withdraws. She retreats—dutifully—into the kitchen, licking her wounds, feeling alone and defeated. She mutters to herself her common chorus, *If only I had a husband who would accept me as I am. I need to be loved unconditionally, not attacked all the time. Supper?* she murmurs. *I'd like to dump this hot pasta right over his hot head.*

CONSIDERING THE CAUSE OF ANGER

How can Jack and Jill learn to handle their sinful anger? Where do they begin the process of changing their outbursts and resentment? As biblical Christians, they know that mere behavioral modification is not enough. Jesus had plenty to say about whitewashed tombs filled with dead bones. Of course Jack and Jill want to end these frequent fights, and replace their sinful words and actions with godly, peaceful behavior. Yet thorough and lasting godly change requires more than outward change. Jack and Jill want, and need, inward change.

To accomplish this change, Jack and Jill must deal with their angry roots. What causes their anger? Our culture offers a myriad of theories. Some theorists think anger flows from deep, inner, unconscious psychodynamic forces. Murky motives lurk within and impulsively drive us.

Others blame anger on past childhood mistreatment. This might include traumatic crises, such as physical beatings or sexual molestation. Or it might result from chronic bad nurturing, such as parental neglect, dysfunctional family dynamics, or wrong parental modeling of anger in many forms. Others argue that present hardships and current circumstantial suffering produce anger. Offenses against us, unmet emotional needs, or living with angry people "make" us mad.

Medical-model proponents see anger arising from physiological factors—fatigue, genetic abnormalities, brain-chemical imbalances, hormone deficiencies, or bodily disabilities. Some Christians root anger in direct satanic activity within us—possession or oppression by the devil or maybe even "demons of anger." And every writer decries the plethora of angry athletes, actors, and other cultural heroes paraded before us as unfit role models. (Pleading "I'm not a role model" doesn't exempt them from their influence on their fans.)

The Bible, of course, recognizes many of these hardships and speaks to them with compassion and robust insight. There is certainly a real devil who lies and deceives. Our outer man is decaying; illnesses and hormonal changes hamper us and become occasions for sin. In our fallen world, people—past and present—do hurt us and abuse us. Moreover, the Bible recognizes that such factors can exert enormous impact. They tempt and provoke us, making anger easy to develop and difficult to control. Every wise counselor knows the impact of these provocations.

> **Our Culture's Theories about the Cause of Anger**
> - Inner, unconscious psychodynamic forces
> - Childhood trauma or chronic bad nurturing
> - Present sufferings
> - Unmet emotional needs
> - Physiological factors
> - Satanic attacks

Yet provocations are not causes. Jack's perpetually angry dad did not *cause* Jack's explosiveness. Jill's "time of the month" makes it harder for her to handle Jack, but it doesn't *make* her bitter. Scripture resists both the reductionism and the determinism implied in those theories. As divine image-bearers, we are not passive machines but active moral responders, accountable to God. We must not allow any of the half dozen types of hardships mentioned above to dehumanize us. We are more than mere reactors. "Garbage in, garbage out" may explain man-made computers' output, but not the behavior of God's image bearers. Jack and Jill, and you and I, are not complex robots but active choosers and responsible free agents before the living Lord.

How, then, can we begin to understand Jack's and Jill's anger? To deal with the problem of anger and conflicts, we must start with the cause. Merely addressing wrong behavior is not enough.

THE REAL CAUSE: THE HEART

What, then, causes evil anger? Scripture provides deeper, richer, more realistic answers than the secular or pseudo-

Christian theories offer: anger comes from the heart. As Jesus said in Mark 7:20–23 "What comes out of a man is what makes him 'unclean.' For from within, out of men's hearts, come evil thoughts, sexual immorality, theft, murder, adultery, greed, malice, deceit, lewdness, envy, slander, arrogance and folly. All these evils come from inside and make a man 'unclean.' "

Or again, in Luke 6:43–45, "No good tree bears bad fruit, nor does a bad tree bear good fruit. Each tree is recognized by its own fruit. People do not pick figs from thornbushes, or grapes from briers. The good man brings good things out of the good stored up in his heart, and the evil man brings evil things out of the evil stored up in his heart. For out of the overflow of his heart his mouth speaks" (cf. Matt. 5:21–22; 15:15–20; Gal. 5:16–21; Heb. 3:12–13; James 1:13–15). The heart of all sin—including sinful anger—is the human heart.

What is the "heart"? It is the most frequent biblical term for a person's entire inner self, an all-encompassing term that includes our thoughts, will, affections, and emotions. Hebrews 4:12 pinpoints two primary functions—our beliefs and motives. God's living, active Word "judges the thoughts and attitudes of the heart."

In other words, sinful anger arises from the sinful beliefs and motives that reign in the unbeliever and remain in the Christian. No wonder Proverbs 4:23 insists, "Above all else, guard your heart, for it is the wellspring of life."

Therefore, to change anger in your heart, you must recognize and uproot your sinful beliefs and motives, and replace them with godly ones. Godly change for Jack and Jill, and for you and me, must occur in the beliefs and motives that underlie our responses.

In *One Day in the Life of Ivan Denisovich*, the Russian writer Alexander Solzhenitsyn pictured this truth in a powerful prison scene. The title character questions how his fellow prisoner Alyosha, a Christian, can cling to a God who leaves him in prison, hungry. Ivan challenges his Christian friend to ask God to provide food. Alyosha's response stuns the skeptics. Instead of asking God for food, Alyosha tells Ivan that they must pray "that the Lord Jesus should remove the scum of anger from our hearts."[1]

ANGER IN THE CHRISTIAN

The apostle addresses ungodly anger in James 4:1–2: "What causes fights and quarrels among you? Don't they come from your desires that battle within you? You want something but don't get it. You kill and covet, but you cannot have what you want. You quarrel and fight. . . ."

James indicts his Christian readers with several forms of angry fruit. He speaks of killing, coveting, quarreling, and fighting. Though the killing may refer to homicide, it more likely alludes to our Lord's comparison, in the Sermon on the Mount, of anger as the moral equivalent of murder (Matt. 5:21–22; cf. 1 John 3:15).

James later adds the related sins of slander and judgmentalism: "Brothers, do not slander one another. Anyone who speaks against his brother or judges him speaks against the law and judges it. When you judge the law, you are not keeping it, but sitting in judgment on it. There is only one Lawgiver and Judge, the one who is able to save and destroy. But you—who are you to judge your neighbor?" (James 4:11–12).

All this, James sadly reports, occurs within the body of Christ, the church! Having had the privilege of assisting severely conflicted churches in several denominations, I can testify that James's first-century descriptions are no less relevant in the twenty-first century. Sinful anger has battered and bruised many parts of Christ's body. As someone has noted, "The Bride's dress is torn."

49

IDENTIFYING ANGER'S HEART CAUSES

How does James tackle these anger expressions? He starts with their cause: "What causes fights and quarrels among you?" (James 4:1a). James is no behaviorist or moralist. Like other biblical writers, he intensely pursues motivation. It is not enough for you to try to cease angry behavior and replace it with godly fruit. You must deal with your heart.

Yet James does not depend on modern psychodynamic or need psychologies to understand human motivation. The cause lies not in esoteric, inaccessible forces lurking within some unconscious inner region of one's soul. James is neither a behaviorist nor a psychoanalyst. And while he calls us to resist the devil in verse 7, he doesn't blame the devil for our sin.

Listen to the apostle's analysis of the heart cause of anger: "Don't they come from your desires that battle within you? You want something but don't get it. You kill and covet, but you cannot have what you want. You quarrel and fight. You do not have, because you do not ask God. When you ask, you do not receive, because you ask with wrong motives, that you may spend what you get on your pleasures" (vv. 1b–3).

Consider four pictures packed into these verses. First, anger arises from our entrenched desires and pleasures that "battle" within us. The Greek verb presents a military image of our desires serving in an army encamped for battle. They are entrenched troops, fixed and positioned to fight, not easily budged or relinquished. Likewise, 1 Peter 2:11 describes the sinful desires "which war against your soul." It is spiritual warfare in the heart, the battle of the flesh versus the Spirit (see Gal. 5:16–26).

Furthermore, our unmet ruling "wants" or "desires" produce anger. As we will see below, the context implies that the problem with these desires is that they rule or control us. In the end, unchecked, they produce sin and death (see James 1:14–15).

Third, anger arises from coveting. Like the previous terms, the verb "covet" may refer to godly seeking or ungodly envying, as in this context. The tenth commandment—"You shall not covet"—uncovers us (Ex. 20:17; Rom. 7:7–11). Grasping, greedy hearts generate conflicts.

Finally, based on verse 3, anger comes from selfish motives. James warns against praying to indulge personal "pleasures." The sinful heart seeks to please itself more than to please God. It craves its own kingdom, not God's. It does not pray in Christ's name according to God's will. No wonder Solzhenitsyn's Alyosha prayed not for parcels or rations, but for God to "remove the scum of anger" from our hearts. And notice both in James 4:3

> **The Heart Causes of Anger: Four Synonyms in James 4:1–3**
> - Entrenched, battling desires and pleasures
> - Unmet ruling wants and desires
> - Coveting and envy
> - Selfish motives (even for good things)

and in Alyosha's case that even prayer can be quickly subverted to selfish ends. The very gift and privilege that God has granted can easily become the means by which our sinful hearts express themselves. And as we'll see in chapter 7, when God doesn't give us what we pray for, we easily become angry at him.

How can we determine whether our desires are sinful? One obvious answer is when we desire a sinful object, i.e., when the item itself is forbidden. To want something that is intrinsically evil or explicitly forbidden is, of course, sinful. But James's insight is more profound. A desire can also be sinful when it is inordinate or selfish. In other words, it is possible to desire a good or legitimate object *too much*. The problem lies not in wanting something but in wanting it too badly. It's not what we want but how much we want it.

Why do we believe this is James's meaning? Because in verse 2 he holds out the possibility that God might grant the desired

51

item (if the readers meet his conditions, etc.). Surely the God of perfect goodness would not bestow an inherently bad item on his followers (see 1:13, 17).

While James does not name the desired object in verses 1–3, some commentaries suggest, based on the language chosen, that the object is money. It certainly fits the context. Money, of course, is not inherently sinful, despite modern misquotes of the Bible that "money is the root of all evil." What 1 Timothy 6:10 actually says is that "the *love* of money is a root of all kinds of evil," and that being "eager for money" leads to apostasy. It is not money but the love of money that is sinful. Money is a good thing; an inordinate desire for it is evil.

What James 4:1–3 teaches, then, is that our anger comes from the sinful desires that rule our hearts. And those desires are often not for bad things, but for good things we want too badly.

AUGUSTINE'S REFLECTIONS ON HIS INFANCY

We have seen *where* sinful anger begins—in the human heart. But *when* does it emerge? When does this problem arise in the human heart? From conception. "Surely I have been a sinner from birth, sinful from the time my mother conceived me" (Ps. 51:5).

St. Augustine understood this dynamic. Listen to his description of his demanding heart—as an infant—in book 1 of *The Confessions of Saint Augustine*.[2] (Parents, let me warn you in advance that the following may revolutionize the way you look at your babies!)

Having gratefully acknowledged God as his ultimate Provider (through his mother and nursemaid), Augustine writes:

Then I knew only to suck, to repose in what pleased, and to cry at what offended my flesh, nothing more.

Afterwards I began to smile, first in my sleep, then waking. So it was told to me of myself, and I believed it, for we see the like in other infants, though of myself I do not remember it. Thus, little by little, I became conscious of where I was and began to express my wishes to those who could content them. . . . So I flung about at random, limbs and voices, making the few signs I could and such as I could, like—though in truth very little like—what I wished. And *when I was not immediately obeyed*, my wishes being harmful to me or unintelligible, then *I was indignant with my elders for not submitting to me*, with those owing me no service, for *not serving me*, and *avenged myself* on them by tears.[3]

What piercing insight into human rage! A tiny infant flinging his arms and legs, inconsolably crying, all driven by revenge against those who did not immediately obey his demanding little heart. A few pages later, Augustine again reflects on his own original sin. Is it an expression of inward goodness, he asks,

even for a while, to cry for what, if given would hurt? Or bitterly to resent that . . . the very authors of my birth did not *serve me*? That many besides, wiser than me, did not *obey* the nod of my good pleasure? To do my best to strike and hurt because commands were not *obeyed*, which would have been obeyed only to my hurt?[4]

Augustine then makes a brilliant observation about our sinful nature: "The weakness then of an infant's limbs, not its will, is its innocence."[5] What makes us call an infant "innocent?" It is his inability to rise up and punch the person who doesn't feed him on demand, not his innocent heart. An infant's heart would throw a right hook if his arms were strong enough. "The weakness then of an infant's limbs, not its will, is its innocence."

Augustine continues by describing the same angry dynamic in the nursing baby boy whose envy keeps him from wanting his foster brother to share his milk supply. "Is that, too, innocence, when the fountain of milk is flowing in rich abundance, not to allow one to share it, one who is in extreme need and whose very life as yet depends on that."[6]

Why make such a big thing over all this? Isn't this just infant immaturity? Augustine answers, "We bear gently with all this, not as being no or slight evils, but because they will disappear as years increase. For, though tolerated now, the very same tempers are utterly intolerable when found in riper years."[7] In other words, childhood "innocence" soon yields to riper adolescent and adult selfishness. When a child's formerly "innocent" limbs become as developed as his always-demanding heart, be ready for fully developed displays of rage!

IS YOUR DESIRE RULING YOU?

If indeed the heart of anger lies in the human heart and its ruling desires, how can you tell whether your desire is ruling you? When have our wants become inordinate? What are some indicators that a good desire has become a bad master?

Several clues can help us. First, a good desire is inordinate when it consumes you, i.e., when you dwell or ruminate on it. Ask yourself these questions: To what topic does your mind drift when it's undirected? What do you think about in your spare time?

Picture a newly hired computer salesman entering this competitive market for the first time. He begins to master every feature of every PC he sells. He reads his firm's market research on his target audience. Every night he devotes extra time researching his competitor's product line. In fact, he is gearing up for his Wednesday-morning sales presentation to a large firm that is a potential client. Question: Can you predict his reaction when his fiancée mentions that she's accepted a dinner invitation for them to her newly married girlfriend's home on Tuesday night? I suspect that it would differ from the response of the established salesman whose desire for new clients is relatively low.

Or perhaps you have looked forward to stopping at the local Baskin-Robbins ice cream store to surprise your family by picking up a gallon of mint chocolate chip, the all-time favorite of you and your family. You look forward not only to the creamy mint flavor and the sweet chocolate bits swirled throughout, but even more to the appreciative looks on your family's faces. As you drive to the store, not only do you think about it, you begin to salivate. Question: How will you respond if you find that the store is out of mint chocolate chip ice cream? I suspect that your response would differ from the person who is content with any flavor.

In addition, a good desire becomes inordinate when you are willing to sin to get it. Do you manipulate others to get the result you want? Do you cry to elicit sympathy or explode to make people fear you?

In our case study, Jack attacks Jill to pressure her to become the mother and homemaker he demands her to be. By alternately threatening and shaming her, he hopes to change her.

Or consider the classic statement of the employee about to lose his job who declares, "I'd do anything to keep this job." His inordinate love for his job makes him easy prey for a host of inducements to lie or cheat that an unethical supervisor might proffer. Contrast that attitude with that of the man whose desire to maintain his job is under control. While he *likes* his job, he does not *live for* his job. Since he does not love his job in some inordinate way, unethical temptations to keep it do not attract him. He rejects the lie that men *find* their identity in their jobs; he knows that his job is merely one place where he *expresses* his identity in Christ.

Finally, and perhaps most commonly, a good desire becomes inordinate when you sin if you don't get what you want. How do you handle it when God sovereignly withholds your heart's desire? When your felt needs remain unmet? Are you learning godly contentment? Or do you feel and show sinful anger, depression, or fear?

> Clues to Detecting an Inordinate Desire
>
> - Does it consume you? Do you dwell on it constantly?
> - Are you willing to sin to get it?
> - Do you sin when you don't get it?

A drive from my former home in Hurricane, West Virginia, to a conference in Pittsburgh several years ago showed me these dynamics in my own heart. The event began on a Friday morning and was scheduled to end on Saturday at noon, allowing me just enough time to return home for our family's Saturday-night celebration of my son's birthday. This desire for the conference to end on time so that I could make the party was a good desire. Conferences should stick to their schedules. It's the *right* thing to do, and in my mind I had a *right* that it be done the right way!

But my good desire quickly became a bad master. As several Saturday-morning segments went overtime, I became a bit nervous. *Will this end on time? Why must the speaker talk on and on?* Soon my nervousness gave way to obsession, as I anxiously checked my watch every ten minutes. It was consuming my mind and distracting me from the worthwhile activities of the conference.

Sadly, things got worse as it now appeared that the conference would end late. I was tempted to forsake my duties as a delegate and leave early. Although I chose to stay till the end, I rushed out the door, rudely avoiding or ignoring the people I could and cutting off in midsentence those I couldn't. I raced like a NASCAR driver to get home on time. In short, I sinned in order to get what I wanted.

But it wasn't over yet. On my way home I found myself resenting the speaker who had gone overtime and the colleagues who had had the gall to actually want to talk to me at the door, delaying my departure (*they should have known I had a four-hour drive!*). I was critical of the conference organizers for their poor planning. In all this, my demanding heart controlled and deceived me.

Can you see these dynamics better in both Jack and Jill? Each got mad when he or she did not get the desired spousal treatment. James's insight is profound. Their demanding hearts were the ultimate cause of their anger. An otherwise legitimate desire becomes an entrenched or ruling desire, even a demand. If unquenched, it produces conflicts, quarrels, and murderous anger. The root of anger lies in unsatisfied ruling "I-wantsies," unmet demands, and fallen heart-idols. Cravings cause conflicts.

BIBLICAL SNAPSHOTS

We see this same heart dynamic in many biblical examples. In Genesis 27, Esau became furious when he failed to get the blessing he wanted from his father, Isaac. He held a grudge against his conniving brother and even plotted his murder. His ruling desire for a good thing—his inheritance that his own brother had stolen—ignited his rage and revenge.

Balaam beat and cursed his donkey because she hindered him from getting what he wanted, i.e., to go to King Balak unchallenged (Num. 22). "You have made a fool of me," cried the prophet in his self-centered anger. Never mind that the hand of God was behind the donkey. "You have made a fool of me"—me, the great me!

Two chapters later, King Balak burned with anger against Balaam (Num. 24). Why? The uncooperative prophet who had awakened to God's command had thwarted the king's desire—his ruling desire—to have his enemy Israel cursed.

Mastered by his own desires, Saul flared up against his own son (1 Sam. 20). He wanted Jonathan to be more devoted to him than to David (and, by extension, to God!). Saul wanted to cling to his kingship and keep down his competitor, David. When Jonathan befriended David, Saul cursed, accused, and hurled his spear at him. While there may be nothing wrong with wanting to preserve one's appointed role, there is everything wrong with seeking to maintain it at all costs. At what cost? Saul's demanding heart ignored God's announcement of his impending removal, and sought to kill the one whom God had raised to replace him. The Pharisees, of course, were to later demonstrate this same heart dynamic, rejecting the Messiah who interfered with their religious rule.

Herod's determination to cling to his kingship led him to murder en masse the infants from whom might spring the "king of the Jews" (Matt. 2). Does this mean that Christ's birth *made* Herod mad? No. Christ's birth occasioned, not caused, Herod's anger. If you asked Herod why he was mad, he might answer, "Because I heard that another King has been born." But Herod's "because" would be untrue: the birth of those baby boys was merely the occasion of his anger, not its cause—the when, not the why. The why lay in his own heart demands to proudly cling to his kingship and get rid of all royal competition.

Luke 4 describes a furious body of Jews at a Nazareth synagogue service. Jesus reminded them how God had graciously saved Gentiles during the days of Elijah and Elisha. Ruled by pride and self-righteousness, these synagogue "worshipers" quickly became inflamed with rage and sought to kill Christ, the very One who fulfilled their own Scriptures.

The silver workers in Ephesus erupted against the apostle Paul because they loved money (Acts 19). They realized that his attack on their idolatry spelled the loss of their profit. When the metal idols in their hands were threatened, the mammon idols in their hearts erupted.

All of these biblical examples—and there are more—reinforce what James 4 teaches us: anger arises when we don't get what we desperately want. Our desires for evil things, or our inordinate desires for even good things, underlie our anger. These are the heart roots of our angry weeds.

Where does your anger begin? God says that it starts in your heart. Remember Grandma Kresge's words, "You've got to get the weeds by the roots, or they'll just grow back." In our next chapter, we will learn how to uproot that anger through biblical repentance.

For Further Reflection and Life Application

1. Read James 3:13–4:12 several times in one sitting and see the apostle James's relentless concern about the heart as the seat of anger. In what various ways does he describe our angry roots?

2. Read through the biblical case studies mentioned in the last section and notice the direct link between the person's demanding heart and his angry actions. Ask God to make you more conscious of this connection in your own life.

3. Notice how often you might think or say sentences that begin with "I need . . ." or "I want . . ." or "I have a right to . . ." Then consider how often the failure to have those desires met makes you angry, or at least irritated or frustrated. By training yourself to become more sensitive to the power of your desires, you are on the road to becoming biblically heart-smart.

4. Pay special attention to those occurrences you would label as "disappointment." While these can at times be the godly experiences of Christian suffering in a

fallen world, they can also reveal ways in which your desires have become inordinate.

5. Keep a written journal of episodes of anger (or of conflict, depression, or frustration, since these are closely linked). The following suggested format may help:

(a) Your Situation: Who, what, where, when? Summarize what happened.

(b) Your Behavior: What did you say, do, and feel in response to what happened? Summarize your words, actions, and emotions, especially the negative ones.

(c) Your Thoughts and Desires: What were you thinking or wanting in the midst of this situation? Summarize your attitudes, thoughts, desires, and motives that might have driven the wrong behavior. Note any "good desire, bad master" dynamics.

REPENTANCE: THE ROAD TO UPROOTING HEART ANGER

In our last chapter, we considered Jack and Jill's marital conflicts; we'll return to their case at the end of this chapter, when we will see the humbling result God brought about.

We saw in chapter 3 that the cause of anger lies in our hearts. Specifically, based on James 4 and supported by a host of other biblical texts, we saw that anger arises from hearts that are ruled by something other than Jesus Christ. We get angry when we don't get what we deeply want. This is even true—and deceptively so—when what we want is not inherently bad. Among Christians, it's often a good thing that we want too much or for selfish reasons.

REBUKES THAT GET TO THE ROOTS

Let me propose a fictional scenario, but one that will hit close to home for many readers: I'm at the end of my workday and preparing to head home. I'm looking forward to seeing my wife and having her greet me warmly when I arrive. As I walk in the front door, I announce, "Hi, dearie; I'm home." I receive no response. I walk to the back of our house and see

Lauren working on our home computer. I repeat my greeting but receive only a flat, expressionless "Oh, it's you; hi," as she continues to type away. My anticipation of being greeted quickly turns to anger.

At this point, several behavioral expressions might emerge, some of which we'll examine in subsequent chapters. Let's consider four. First, I might yell at my wife. I might even charge into the back office with an in-your-face stance. I might tell her how she has failed me, how "the least you can do after I work all day is to get up and greet me," how "really good wives like Sally or Cindy" greet their husbands.

On the other hand, I might respond in the opposite way. I might walk away and go to my little home office—retreating to my cave—to engage in some seemingly deserved self-pity. *If she wants to talk to me, she can crawl to me.* After all, I'm the king, and King Bob can grant admittance to his royal throne room to whomever he wants. It's all up to me. I can receive her, or I can dismiss her, sending her away with a cold shoulder.

Alternatively, from my same cave, I could pick up the phone and call my buddy Doug and "share" (good Christians like me don't "gossip") Lauren's behavior with him. "Doug, she did it again. I work hard all day, and all I ask is that she might greet me at the door. And what do I get? Nothing! Nada! Zilch!" And then I add a closing whine: "All I want is to be greeted by my wife; is that so bad?" Doug, of course, plays his usual "support" role. He listens to me, commiserates with me, assures me that my desire is legitimate and that I deserve to be greeted, and joins me in my prosecution of my wife. In fact, Doug confides with me some of his own similar frustrations with his wife, and pretty soon we are engaged in that familiar game of "can you top this?" Before long, we have all the makings of a support group for "Husbands Whose Wives Don't Greet Them at the Door." We might even hit the talk-show circuit and start 12-step HWWDGTAD groups all over the country.

But my options continue. A fourth sinful step I might take is to pick up that same telephone and this time, instead of calling my friend, call Lauren's friend. "Donna? Hi, Bob here. Listen, can you talk to Lauren for me? I come home every day, and she never greets me. . . . But she'll listen to you, Donna. Give her some of that biblical counsel about being a loving wife found in that book you read. You know, the one about meeting your husband's emotional needs, or filling up his love thermos, or whatever it was called."

Now, it's obvious that all four of these responses are wrong. In fact, a faithful brother in Christ might rebuke me for each one. "Bob, you know it's not right to chase down your wife and yell at her. Jesus commands you to cherish and nourish her, not blast and bombard her. That's not the way Jesus treats you." Ashamed, I hang my head and repent. "You're right, brother; I've sinned. O God, please forgive me."

"Furthermore, Bob," my faithful friend continues, "the way you pulled away from your wife and holed up in your cave is not the way Christ loved his bride. He moved toward her in Ephesians 5. He came near, not pulled away." Ashamed, I hang my head and repent. "You're right, brother; I've sinned. O God, please forgive me."

"And Bob," he concludes, "you know that complaining to your buddy Doug is gossip, and asking her friend Donna to intervene is manipulative. Instead of overlooking minor offenses, or going to her to deal with your problem, the way Matthew 5 and Matthew 18 instruct you, you are involving others who aren't part of the problem." Again, I hang my head in shame and repent. "You're right, brother; I've sinned. O God, please forgive me."

How might we assess my friend's ministry? It had many marks of Christlike friendship. He cared enough about me to confront me. He confronted me in love to help me. He used

Scripture, not just his own personal opinion. He connected me to God.

Yet something is missing from my friend's counsel. It is helpful but insufficient. What is lacking? He hasn't confronted my heart. He hasn't gone after the James 4 issues. In particular, he hasn't rebuked my ruling heart desire to be greeted by my wife, that inordinate root desire for a good thing that has produced the sinful fruit.

GOD'S GRACE: HOPE FOR ANGRY HEARTS

Let's see how God graciously seeks to uproot our sinful desires. Thankfully, James 4 does more than diagnose sinful desires. God's Word gives hope and help to Jack and Jill, and to you and me. In what do that help and hope consist? The grace of God! Listen to James's answer in verse 6: "But he [God] gives more grace. That is why Scripture says, 'God opposes the proud but gives grace to the humble.' "

Notice that God's answer for anger does not come from a set of action steps or self-help tips. James's answer for angry hearts is not "how-to" but "Whom-to": we must go to God himself. As one biblical counselor and author, David Powlison, has observed, "James' solution to interpersonal conflict is shockingly vertical."[1] Verse 6 points us to God as the One who supplies grace for angry idolaters. He "gives us more grace"; he "gives grace to the humble."

What kind of grace do we need? Certainly we need God's *forgiving grace*, his mercy in Christ that pardons all our sins (Heb. 4:16; 1 John 1:8–2:2). Our anger—in both heart and behavior—is evil. Yet thankfully Jesus provides abundant pardon. His atoning fountain never runs dry. His blood never wears thin or expires. There is mercy even for angry idolaters.

Reader, don't minimize this provision. Once you see the depth of your anger—the angry roots, not merely the angry fruits—you will discover that you need a bigger Savior than you thought. You will need a Savior big enough to forgive big sinners—sinners who sin inwardly in their demanding hearts, not just outwardly with their critical tongues. Praise God that we have such a towering Redeemer.

Yet we also need God's *enabling grace*, the grace that empowers us to be and do what he wants us to be and do. It is divine grace to "help us in our time of need" (Heb. 4:16). It is powerful grace that is "sufficient" in times of weakness (2 Cor. 12:9–10). His grace enables us to forgive those people whose offenses would otherwise provoke anger. It empowers us to progressively overcome long-term patterns of judgmentalism, venting, and clamming. God's grace nourishes, guides, and strengthens us even when our bad circumstances continue.

OUR RESPONSE: REPENTING OF ANGRY HEART DESIRES

How should we respond to this God's glorious offer of grace to angry people? James 4 uses a host of metaphors to call for thorough heart repentance. In verses 4–5, God calls us to reject our worldly lovers. "You adulterous people, don't you know that friendship with the world is hatred toward God? Anyone who chooses to be a friend of the world becomes an enemy of God. Or do you think Scripture says without reason that the spirit he caused to live in us tends toward envy . . . ?"

The apostle summons the Old Testament imagery of spiritual adultery to call us to abandon our sinful demandingness. While the world's false counsel and vain charms cannot cause sin, they shape and stimulate our desires in powerful ways. Jack's and Jill's flirtations with their own heart demands—what they wrongly think they *must* have from each other—jeopardize their fidelity to God and to each other. James pleads with us to stop befriending and bedding down with lies.

In verses 6–10, God calls us to repent of our sinful ruling desires. James issues a rapid-fire series of specific commands:

> That is why Scripture says: "God opposes the proud but gives grace to the humble." Submit yourselves, then, to God. Resist the devil, and he will flee from you. Come near to God and he will come near to you. Wash your hands, you sinners, and purify your hearts, you double-minded. Grieve, mourn and wail. Change your laughter to mourning and your joy to gloom. Humble yourselves before the Lord, and he will lift you up.

We must humble ourselves before God. The repetition of "humble" in the beginning and end forms a literary *inclusio*—a pair of bookends—that brackets this section. We must forsake the "my rights, my kingdom, my will" type of pride that spawns anger.

One morning my wife and I were setting up our unused crib to host some good friends. They and their new baby were coming to visit us for several days. Armed with our screwdrivers, she on the right and I on the left, we pressed on to complete our task.

As Lauren finished her side, she noticed that I was having a problem. I was making little progress (we later discovered that the screw hole was stripped). She leaned over to innocently ask if she could help. I snapped at her angrily, "No, I don't need any help!" and went on with my fruitless labor, discharging steam from both reddening ears. We eventually finished the task together, in cold silence.

I reflected on that episode later that day. *Why had I snapped at her? Why the sharp words? Why the rising temperature?* As I examined my heart, God the great Surgeon was already guiding his scalpel. I realized that my anger had come from twin sinful ruling desires: *I must be in control of this project, and I must be seen as the competent one. She, and others, must view me as the "man of the house," the one who can swiftly and skillfully screw in any screw (faster than a speeding bullet, of course) and handle any "manly" maintenance task.*

Thankfully, God showed me my folly and the pride of my beliefs. I had imbibed a false standard, an unbiblical definition of headship and masculinity. Other men were skillful handymen, including Lauren's dad; I must be also. Such legalism enslaved me and generated my anger. The craving to appear competent—according to my standards—controlled me.

By God's grace, I humbled myself and came to see that true manliness does not consist in socially determined roles. It involves building up and encouraging my wife. It also means taking responsibility for household tasks, improving my handyman skills where I can, and learning with my wife—together—how to reassemble cribs. I sought her forgiveness, and we reconciled the tension. We even had a good laugh later: we both agreed that I should not quit my day job to become a carpenter!

Returning to James 4, we see in verse 7 that repentance includes submitting to God and coming near to him. You must "wash your hands" and "purify your hearts"—another way to describe both behavioral and internal, or "fruit and root" repentance. The weeds of anger must be uprooted. James rightly views angry Christians as saved sinners who need ongoing repentance. Like Paul in Romans 7, we are double-minded people with loyalties divided between God and self/idols (James 1:6–8). We must grieve, mourn, and wail. Repentance is serious business and issues forth in emotional sorrow over sin.

Verse 7 puts it another way: "Resist the devil, and he will flee from you." Like the world, the devil does not *cause* our anger but stimulates the sinful desires—our flesh—that do cause it (note the very tight connection between our sinful hearts and Satan in Ephesians 2:1–3; 4:26–27; James 3:15). Both sin and Satan seek to devour us (Gen. 4:7; 1 Peter 5:8).

While it is erroneous to blame Satan for our anger, it is naive to isolate him from it. Both activities are dangerous.

What is our mode of warfare against the devil? Note the operative verb "resist," the most frequent command in the epistles for the mode of warfare against him (see also Eph. 6:10–18; 1 Peter 5:8–9). Neither James nor any other epistle writer commands us to exorcise or rebuke the devil or his demons.

What does it mean to resist the devil? The context of each passage yields answers. We resist Satan in James 4:7 by drawing near to God in humble submission, faith, and repentance. In 1 Peter 5:6–9, we resist him by standing firm in faith, by exercising self-control and spiritual watchfulness, by humbling ourselves before the Lord, and by casting our anxieties on him. And Ephesians 6:10–18 calls us to resist by putting on, and standing firm in, our Christian armor of faith, righteousness, truth, and prayer.

To resist the devil, then, means identifying and rejecting his lies. Resisting entails exposing and withstanding his temptations. It means resting in our Savior-Advocate, Jesus Christ the Righteous One, amid Satan's accusations. It involves repenting of the flesh and refusing to follow the devil's angry example and murderous will. It means a different agenda for both Jack as he heads home and Jill as she anticipates his arrival.

Finally, in verses 11–12, God calls you to resign your God-playing and refuse to usurp his sole prerogatives:

> Brothers, do not slander one another. Anyone who speaks against his brother or judges him speaks against the law and judges it. When you judge the law, you are not keeping it, but sitting in judgment on it. There is only one Lawgiver and Judge, the one who is able to save and destroy. But you—who are you to judge your neighbor?

In one sense, all sin reflects God-playing. The first sinful act arose from Adam and Eve's desire to be like God (Gen. 3:1–6). Murder usurps God's right to give and take life. Stealing seizes his right to distribute material blessings as he wills.

What about anger or slander? As a form of judgmentalism— a negative moral judgment against perceived evil—these are also God-playing. We usurp his rights. How so? It starts when we legislate required behavior for another.[2] We may or may not choose to tell the other person. For example:

- When thou drivest thine automobile, thou shalt not turn to the left or to the right in front of me, except thou signalest thine intention to do so with thy turn signal.
- Thou shalt not let the sun go down on my phone call or e-mail, but thou shalt return it today, while it is still called today.
- Thou shalt love me the way I want to be loved, with thy whole heart, soul, mind, and strength.

If you break one of my statutes, I log your violation in my mental record book. I may or may not present the evidence to you, depending on my preference (after all, I can do whatever I want in my imaginary world in which I divinely reign!). In either case, I am both the star witness and the chief prosecutor against you. Moreover, I play both judge and executioner. I sound the gavel, pronounce you guilty, sentence you to whatever punishment lies within my power, and mete out justice.

What does repentance look like? I throw away my statute book. I drop the charges. I cover your offenses with the blanket of Christian love and erase them from my ledger. I lay down my gavel, descend my judicial bench, and remove my black robe. I refuse to punish you but instead begin to love you.

What about the serious sins that people commit against us? God calls us to rebuke such offenders and perhaps go the next step in summoning the civil or church authorities. Yet even here we must ultimately entrust such perpetrators to God's just hands. We must learn to let him be the lawgiver, recorder, witness, prosecutor, judge, and executioner. He calls us to trust in his perfect justice. He will condemn the guilty and vindicate the righteous in his time and his manner. He hasn't deputized us.

OWNING YOUR GUILT AND RECEIVING GOD'S GRACE

Do you remember the truth of James 4:6? God "gives us more grace. That is why Scripture says: 'God opposes the proud but gives grace to the humble.' " To receive God's forgiving grace, you must own your anger. God opposes the proud but gives grace to the humble. We must not blame past or present circumstances. We are responsible. It is no innocent matter to obey selfish desires, to march to the beat of the world and its evil ruler, and to dethrone Almighty God. Our own hearts cause our anger. As Proverbs 28:13 declares, "He who conceals his sins does not prosper, but whoever confesses and renounces them finds mercy."

What does blame-shifting sound like? "I got angry *because* he yelled at me." This reveals the occasion but not the real cause of anger—my ruling desire for fair treatment. Consider the functional view of man imbedded in these common complaints:

- "She made me so angry."
- "My kids push my buttons."
- "The devil did a number on me."
- "I got my dad's temper."
- "It's not me but the booze talkin'."
- "I get this way every month because of PMS."

Each of these statements implies that we are passive victims or machines, subject to another person's (or thing's) control. One of my favorite cartoons cleverly illustrates this tendency. Two panel-chested robots—a husband and wife—sit in the office of a human marriage therapist. The caption quotes the counselor: "I can see that both of you are extremely adept at pushing each other's buttons."

Against this view, the Bible portrays us as active moral agents—made in God's image—responsible for our own behavior. We must not blame our family members, our friends, our genes, our parents, our church leaders, society, our hormones, or the devil for our anger.

Instead, as we humble ourselves before God and confess that our anger is our own, arising from idolatrous lies and lusts, we find God's forgiving, enabling grace. We must meet God, draw near to God, have dealings with God, submit to God, and bring our anger to God. We must shift our functioning faith from worthless heart-idols to God's Son.

We begin by identifying the ruling desire. Writing it out is a helpful step. "I am angry now because I wrongly think that I must have a husband who _____." Then repent, not of the desire itself, but of the rulingness of the desire, of the way you have been letting it control your heart. Ask God for his forgiving and enabling grace. And consciously submit this desire to God's sovereignty, goodness, and wisdom. Then consciously seek by prayer and meditation to look above it with a greater desire to know and love God, live out the implications of the cross, and serve others.

KING DADDY OR SERVANT DADDY?

What happens as we commune with God? He assures us that he, not we, will judge evildoers and vindicate his people. And we meet him as our own merciful Savior and the sovereign Father committed to his eternal glory and our eternal good. This God of all grace floods us with deepening repentance and renewed faith.

In the early days of my pastorate, I supplemented my income by painting houses. One week I had a painting job in a town thirty minutes away. I started on a Monday and worked an eleven-hour day. By the end of the first night, I was exhausted and hungry. I arrived home at 8:00 p.m. filled with my own wants: *I must have supper ready for me and served to me by my wife. I must have kids who will leave me alone and let me relax. King Daddy has arrived; all bow!*

Like Jack in our case above, when those demands failed to be realized I became angry. Why? What lies did I believe? The world, in my God-playing universe, should revolve around me. My wife and children were moons made to orbit around me, the sun. Lauren existed to provide me with supper and with tranquility. My sons were to follow my decrees and ordinances, and dutifully refrain from interrupting the king at rest. As you might guess, my family and I had a miserable evening.

I drove home along the same route the following night, as hungry and tired as before. Yet this time it was different. God met me in prayer. He stunned me with a simple text, Mark 10:45: "For even the Son of Man did not come to be served, but to serve, and to give his life as a ransom for many."

Through that single verse, God laid my whole agenda before my eyes. Would I be like my Savior or like those who killed him? Would I seek to be served or to serve? Whose pleasure was I seeking? "For even Christ did not please himself . . ." (Rom. 15:3).

What happened that night? I drew near to God and he drew near to me. My encounter with the Son of Man changed me. Having repented of self-centeredness, and now poised with a new goal of Christlike service, I was blessed with an evening of peace and joy with my family. I submitted my desires for food and tranquility to God's greater desires, i.e., for me to be a godly lover and servant of my family. King Daddy was exiled; Servant Daddy had arrived. Instead of "King Daddy has come; all bow," the evening theme became "Servant Daddy is here; be glad!"

The problem I had that first night is the problem we raised in the fictional scenario at the beginning of this chapter. The desire to be greeted at the door can so rule someone's heart that, when it is not met, it can produce all sorts of anger expressions. But the Mark 10:45 text quoted above exposes the real problem: wanting to be greeted, not to greet! In fact, we might paraphrase our Lord's words this way: "For even the Son of Man did not come to *be greeted*, but to *greet*, and to give his life as a ransom for many."

JACK'S AND JILL'S REPENTANCE

In Jesus Christ, angry people find a Savior perfectly suited to meet their deepest needs for pardoning mercy and powerful hope. He died and rose to conquer your anger. His Word has answers. His Spirit has resources. His church has wisdom. You can reject the world, repent of your ruling desires, resist Satan, and resign your God-playing. He gives us more grace!

How did these truths about God and his grace affect Jack the angry yeller and Jill the angry retreater? Thankfully, they transformed their hearts. Let's close this chapter by listening to their repentance. Note particularly their newfound, discriminating, James 4 awareness of the evil desires driving their anger:

Jack: "Lord, you know that I'd like a wife who will keep a cleaner house, manage the kids better, and show more sexual interest. But I don't *have* to have these things. I realize that in Christ I don't need them, although I often live as though I do.

73

The desire for these things so often rules me. That's why I criticize Jill. That's why I rant and rave. Lord, I have been obeying the world, the flesh, and the devil.

"Father, forgive me. I have been soaking up the world's lies. Help me to reject them. I've cooperated with the devil, who is driving a wedge between my wife and me. Help me to resist him. Above all, I've played God. I've usurped your throne by demanding that my kingdom come and my will be done.

"Thank you for the blood of Jesus your Son that paid for all my sins—both my hotheaded words and my idolatrous desires. Thank you that he died and rose for sinners like me. Thank you for his Spirit, who enables me to love Jill the way Christ loved the church and gave himself up for her in sacrificial death. Help me, dear Lord, to die to self and live for you. Help me to love Jill with your kind of love. Be with me tonight as I seek her forgiveness. Amen."

Jill: "Lord, you know how much I'd like a husband who is more gentle and patient, and less critical. I am sure that's what you want Jack to be. But that's between you and him. Lord, I've sinned. My craving for these things has made me a sour, cold, bitter wife. I'd like Jack to change, but I don't need him to change. With your help I can be a gentle, Christlike wife.

"Father, I see that I have taken your role as lawgiver, prosecutor, judge, and executioner. I have decreed that Jack must love me the way I want to be loved. I've been keeping a record of his sins and replaying them every day, all day, in my mind. I've judged and declared him guilty. And I've imposed my sentence by withdrawing from him and criticizing him around my friends. I've dragged my feet when he has asked me to do a better job with the house and kids.

"I now see how subtle and wicked I have been. I've believed the world's lies—even those found in some "Christian" self-help books—about what wives need. I've yielded to Satan's temptations, and I am sorry.

"Forgive me, Lord, for my many sins, especially those in my heart. Thank you for sending Jesus to die for me. Help me to live for him. Help me to rest in his righteousness. Help me to submit my desires, even the good ones, to you. Help me to forgive Jack as you have forgiven me. Help me to be a wife who pleases you and serves my husband. Amen."

For Further Reflection and Life Application

1. The next time you find yourself angry at someone, note your temptation to blame the person, the situation, the devil, or even your own tiredness or physical condition, and thus bypass your own heart. Whom or what do you typically blame? Remember the warnings of James 1:13–15; 3:13–16; and 4:1–3. Often a pastor, elder, or mature Christian friend can help you see those blind spots.

2. Memorize Mark 10:45. The next time someone fails to treat you the way you want to be treated, use the Mark 10:45 servanthood principle to ask whether you are more driven to be served or to serve. For example, if someone fails to keep a promise or fails to return your phone call or e-mail, use it as an opportunity to recall whether you yourself have failed to do the same toward someone.

3. Continue the same journaling activity recommended at the end of chapter 3, but add the fourth item listed below:
   (a) Your Situation: Who, what, where, when? Summarize what happened.
   (b) Your Behavior: What did you say, do, and feel in response to what happened? Summarize your

words, actions, and emotions, especially the negative ones.

(c) Your Thoughts and Desires: What were you thinking or wanting in the midst of this situation? Summarize your attitudes, thoughts, desires, and motives
that might have driven the wrong behavior. Note
any "good desire, bad master" dynamics.

(d) God's Answers: How does God want you to deal
with this situation now or the next time it occurs?
What changes in your behavior and in your
thoughts, desires, and motives seem needed? What
steps should you take to uproot that anger?

4. Memorize James 4:6. Daily ask God to teach and pour
out into you both his forgiving and enabling grace,
that you might wisely handle those situations that typically provoke you to anger. When your angry heart
rises inside, remember his promise to oppose the proud
but give grace to you who humble yourself.

5. Review Jack's and Jill's prayers above and highlight
how they have come to see that their anger was idolatrous—playing God, heeding the voice of his enemy,
and placing people or things above him. Use their
prayers to encourage your own repenting and communing with God in prayer.

5

CHANGING OUR ANGRY BEHAVIOR: SINFUL REVEALING

J ack and Jill have come a long way since their Thursday night fight. They have learned that thorough and lasting godly change begins in the heart. Angry words and actions arise from selfish beliefs and motives. Sinful roots produce sinful fruits. The Lord has used passages such as James 4 to expose their sinful desires, elicit their wholehearted repentance, and escort them into communion with the God of forgiving, enabling grace.

But this is just the beginning. Behavioral change must accompany heart change. How do Jack and Jill change their angry behavior?

Let's recall their actions. Jack revealed his anger by aiming his tongue at his wife and his fist at the wall. He vented and exploded. Why? Not because he was constitutionally some uncontrollable pot of boiling water, but because he wanted to make his point known and felt by all within the house. *You all need to listen to me.* In other words, he believed that revealing his anger this way would gain his goal. *Maybe Jill will feel bad enough about her failures to change.* Jack yelled in order to win the conflict.

Jill, on the other hand, concealed her anger against Jack. She was equally furious, but she did not rant and rave. Instead,

7

she hid her anger from Jack by retreating into the other room. There she and her green beans simmered away.

It is important to note that at other times, and toward other people, the tactics would reverse. Jill would occasionally blast Jack and her kids. Jack would seethe with a mixture of guilt and anger underneath his outwardly composed exterior, particularly when he got angry with his boss.

How should we evaluate their angry behavior, and how can we help them, and ourselves, put off their sinful practices?

To answer such a sweeping question, let's first consider a way to organize types of angry behavior. Since Scripture supplies no simple typology—it defies such partitioning—we cannot be dogmatic in creating categories. How might we slice the pie in ways that encompass the biblical data?

The most popular approach among both secular and Christian counselors views angry behavior either as ventilating (or blowing up) or as internalizing (clamming up). Venters explode; clammers stuff. Venters blow their lids; clammers quietly stew inside, underneath their lids. (At some point the clammer might blow, but not necessarily.) While this basic division is helpful, its focus on mere behavior may miss the intentionality behind the action. Moreover, there are many self-controlled ways (e.g., calculating revenge) by which one might outwardly express anger without blowing steam. In addition, the venting and clamming metaphors may suggest that anger is a kind of fluid that must somehow be released or drained.[1]

Perhaps a more helpful way to categorize anger responses is to think of ways in which a person might either reveal his anger or conceal his anger. People choose either to express their anger (sometimes by venting) or to hide their anger.[2] We engage in overt or in covert operations. Revealing methods consist of various ways we let others know and feel our anger. Concealing tactics hide our anger from others, though the anger itself remains.

Both strategies, of course, are sinful. Both revealing anger and concealing anger offend God and sabotage relationships, and call for specific biblical steps of correction and replacement. This chapter focuses on sinful revealing; the next addresses sinful concealing.

How do we control and correct sinful anger expressions and replace them with Christlike words and actions? What directives does God's Word give to us?

We hardly need to describe the ways people reveal anger. We have heard it too often in ourselves and others: angry mouths, loud voices, sharp tongues, undeleted expletives. We have also witnessed it: flying fists, slammed doors, people walking out of a meeting. There is no limit to the ways in which we let others know we are upset.

BIBLICAL EXAMPLES OF REVEALED ANGER

In chapter 1, we considered several cases of revealed anger in the Bible. Let's survey several more. Genesis 39 records Joseph's mistreatment at the hands of Potiphar and his wife. She solicited and approached Joseph sexually. Although he refused and ran, she accused him of attempted rape. Sadly, Potiphar listened to his wife's trumped-up charges. In blind rage, he misjudged the situation and wrongly punished Joseph. Potiphar "burned with anger" against Joseph and threw his choice servant into prison without a trial (vv. 19–20).

Moses revealed his sinful anger in Numbers 20:6–12. Unlike the similar instance forty years prior in Horeb (Ex. 17:1–7), God told him not to strike the rock but merely to speak to it, and water would pour forth. Yet here at Kadesh, in anger, Moses struck the rock and uttered rash words (Ps. 106:32–33). God in turn rebuked him for unbelief and for dishonoring him before the people. God did not applaud Moses for getting his

79

anger off his chest; he judged him severely. Anger, as we have seen, is a moral matter, done before the eyes of God.

Matthew 2:1–18 recalls King Herod's deceitful schemes to search and destroy his newborn royal competitor, "the king of the Jews." When his efforts were unsuccessful, his anger rose to dastardly heights. He did not try to conceal his rage: "When Herod realized that he had been outwitted by the Magi, he was furious, and he gave orders to kill all the boys in Bethlehem and its vicinity who were two years old and under, in accordance with the time he had learned from the Magi" (v. 16). His evil heart determination to cling to his kingship eventually produced mass murder.

BIBLICAL PRECEPTS AGAINST REVEALED ANGER

Scripture not only gives us examples of such sinful anger, but also records directives and warnings against it. In the Sermon on the Mount, Jesus drew the same connection between anger and murder that Herod's case illustrated. He declared in Matthew 5:21–22:

> You have heard that it was said to the people long ago, "Do not murder, and anyone who murders will be subject to judgment." But I tell you that anyone who is angry with his brother will be subject to judgment. Again, anyone who says to his brother, "Raca," is answerable to the Sanhedrin. But anyone who says, "You fool!" will be in danger of the fire of hell.

Two observations are in order. First, Jesus recognized anger as the moral equivalent of murder. Heart anger is the seedbed for homicide. Both reflect failures to love God and one's neighbor. The apostle John concurs: "Anyone who hates his brother is a murderer, and you know that no murderer has eternal life in him" (1 John 3:15). Second, anger in the heart typically

80

comes out in curses from the lips. Proverbs 4:23–24 makes the same causal connection between our heart and our speech (cf. Matt. 12:33–37; 15:17–20; Luke 6:43–45).

In Ephesians 4:17–32, the apostle Paul describes the radical change that Christ's salvation brings, contrasting the new convert's new life with his old life. Part of that new-life change is the call to put off the "old" (sinful) ways and replace them with "new" (righteous) ways. In verses 29–32, he summarizes various revealed forms of evil behavior:

> [29]Do not let any unwholesome talk come out of your mouths, but only what is helpful for building others up according to their needs, that it may benefit those who listen. [30]And do not grieve the Holy Spirit of God, with whom you were sealed for the day of redemption. [31]Get rid of all bitterness, rage and anger, brawling and slander, along with every form of malice. [32]Be kind and compassionate to one another, forgiving each other, just as in Christ God forgave you.

Our rotten words fail to edify others (v. 29) and grieve God's Spirit (v. 30). This grieving of the Spirit is further described in verse 31. Paul ransacks his thesaurus to delineate a putrid pot of anger sins, including such outward forms as rage, brawling, and slander. This sinful anger contradicts the Christlike kindness, forgiveness, and love that should mark God's people (4:32–5:2).

These instructions from our Lord and his apostle, along with the case-study examples above, warn us of the dangers of angry words and actions. Such revelations of rage dishonor our Lord and destroy our neighbors.

OBSERVATIONS ABOUT ANGER FROM PROVERBS

The book of Proverbs contains the richest deposit of warnings and instructions against revealed anger in all of Scripture.

81

It pulls together in graphic form the insights we have already seen in the narrative and didactic forms. Further, its piercing labels and striking metaphors make it especially valuable in persuading us and the ones we're serving to change. Let's absorb its insights as we walk through some key portions.

Proverbs 10 and 12 are clustered with references to godly and ungodly speech. These two chapters furnish fine materials for Bible study about the tongue.

Perhaps the most gripping words in these chapters come in Proverbs 12:18, a verse that every counselor and venting counselee should memorize and feed on: "Reckless words pierce like a sword, but the tongue of the wise brings healing."

The warning is graphic: angry words cut deep. The same "macho" Jack who would never hit a woman has sliced his wife many times with his tongue. This text also puts to death the childhood couplet, "Sticks and stones may break my bones, but names will never hurt me."

Yet the invitation of this text is tantalizing. Jack can—just as you and I can—learn to love others through his speech. We can minister to our families with our tongues. Our words can bind up wounded neighbors and bandage mangled lives. This put-off/put-on agenda of Proverbs 12:18 can and must become a high priority for us.

How does God view a person who reveals his anger? He is not only a violent man (Matt. 5:21–22; Prov. 12:18). Proverbs 14:16–17 calls him a fool and a hothead:

> A wise man fears the Lord and shuns evil, but a fool is hot-headed and reckless. A quick-tempered man does foolish things, and a crafty man is hated.

Unlike our English term, a "fool" in the book of Proverbs is not a jovial clown but an ungodly man. His behavior does not invite laughs, but pity and punishment. Such a text becomes powerful when angry people own such titles for themselves. When a raging revealer such as Jack begins to see himself as God sees him, and calls himself a "venter" or "hothead," he begins to take his sin seriously. He is ready to become "a wise man [who] fears the LORD and shuns evil."

A further descriptor of those who reveal sinful anger is impatience. Later in the same chapter, the wisdom writer observes:

> A patient man has great understanding, but a quick-tempered man displays folly. A heart at peace gives life to the body, but envy rots the bones. (14:29–30)

When asked in session one for his explanation of why he exploded, Jack quickly declared, "I have no patience." While he did not yet see all his heart-idols, he understood this verse. He demanded his family to be what he wanted them to be, immediately. He not only wanted *what* he wanted. He wanted what he wanted *when* he wanted it. Jack neither grasped God's providential dealings nor considered his wife's and children's own life struggles. His expectations, coupled with his impatience, ignited his tirades.

Verse 30 uncovers another dynamic operating in Jack's life, i.e., the biblical connection between such anger/impatience and psychosomatic problems (see chapter 10). His high blood pressure, churning stomach, and constant edginess—his "nerves," as he called them—were symptoms of his sin. As he learned to put off anger and live at peace, his soul and body enjoyed renewed health.

The fifteenth chapter of Proverbs gives a pair of verses essential for wise anger management:

> A gentle answer turns away wrath, but a harsh word stirs up anger. (15:1)

> A hot-tempered man stirs up dissension, but a patient man calms a quarrel. (15:18)

Notice the put-on qualities contrasted with anger. We must learn both gentleness and patience (both fruit of the Spirit in Gal. 5:22–23). In doing so, we promote peace. When we fail to respond in godly ways, we provoke anger from others. Conflict escalates. Calmness evaporates. Clamor erupts. Jack learned this the hard way. Instead of creating a peaceful home, his tirades only stirred the family flames and incited domestic dissension. Venters beget venters. As with Proverbs 12:18 above, 15:1 is a vital verse for every believer to know and meditate on.

Proverbs 29:11 gives a third "must" verse for serious reflection and application:

> A fool gives full vent to his anger, but a wise man keeps himself under control.

The text imbeds several summary truths. As "fools," venters need to own this identity statement as a first step of repentance. They must instead pursue paths of true wisdom, that wisdom anchored in "the fear of the LORD" (Prov. 1:7; 9:10). To vent one's anger is a moral matter. It is to ignore God and despise his Word. Change comes as the angry person heeds God's voice (Prov. 1:20–33) and digs for his truth (Prov. 2:1–8).

Proverbs 29:11 highlights one specific quality of godly wisdom, an ingredient lacking in anger-revealers: self-control. Self-control must replace venting. The anger-revealer must learn to muzzle his mouth, as Proverbs 29:20 cautions:

> Do you see a man who speaks in haste? There is more hope for a fool than for him.

Hasty speech—including its reckless, angry forms—is visible to onlookers. Sadly, there is little prospect of blessing from God apart from repentance. How often you and I have heard—worse, *said*—words we later regret. Jack often did. "You're lazy!" he would tell Jill. "Why did I ever marry you?" Afterward, he was filled with remorse over his hasty, hurtful words. Part of God's agenda for Jack was to repent of his character-assassinating tongue and to speak words that ministered to Jill (Eph. 4:29).

Proverbs 16:32 and 25:28 provide a pair of arresting word pictures that contrast anger with patience and self-control:

> Better a patient man than a warrior, a man who controls his temper than one who takes a city. (16:32)

True strength in God's eyes means victory over one's temper more than one's enemies. The humble follower of Christ is more powerful than the latest television superhero or professional boxer. The "tough guy" who explodes with loud words or pounding fists knows nothing of true strength. Before God, he is a moral wimp.

The second metaphor is equally striking:

> Like a city whose walls are broken down is a man who lacks self-control. (25:28)

Ancient Near Eastern cities depended on stone walls to shield themselves from raiding bandits, vicious wolves, conquering armies, and the like. In the same way, people must realize that uncontrolled venting invites invasions from their spiritual enemies. The angry man or woman is easy prey for the world, the flesh, and the devil.

Jack came to see this truth. While he came to counseling to deal with a specific problem, his anger, he recognized that his whole life was in shambles. He felt far from God and unable to pray. He had begun to drink heavily and to expose himself to soft-core pornography. Jack was a city with broken-down walls. Counseling involved rebuilding the walls of self-control in several key areas.

Jack also came to see the impact that his revealed anger made on others.

> An angry man stirs up dissension, and a hot-tempered one commits many sins. (Prov. 29:22)

In Jack's case, the old expression, "if the shoe fits, wear it," fit his foot all to well. Moreover, to borrow another maxim, that same foot was a foot he too frequently "put in his mouth."

Vented anger wreaks havoc on the people and situations it touches. Produced by sinful desires, it in turn produces more sin (cf. the desire–sin–death progression in James 1:14–15). Jack's angry storming affected the climate of his home.

One specific consequence of Jack's anger helped bring him to counseling. His anger was becoming contagious. When little Johnny began to yell at his mom, Jack and Jill saw the hard truth of Proverbs 22 staring them in the face:

> Do not make friends with a hot-tempered man, do not associate with one easily angered, or you may learn his ways and get yourself ensnared. (22:24–25)

Jack was inadvertently teaching his son his own hot-tempered ways. Johnny simply followed suit.

What else does Proverbs teach anger-revealers? Along with patience and self-control, they need to learn to overlook and forgive the sins that other people commit against them.

A man's wisdom gives him patience; it is to his glory to over-look an offense. (Prov. 19:11)

Venters react in haste to mistreatment; patient disciples respond with forgiveness. "Love covers a multitude of sins" (1 Peter 4:8; cf. Prov. 10:12).

Proverbs also directs us how to deal with anger-venters, beyond the general commands to rebuke and instruct them. We must not try to protect enraged people from the negative repercussions that God may providentially use to wake them up. Venting one's anger incurs consequences:

A hot-tempered man must pay the penalty; if you rescue him, you will have to do it again. (Prov. 19:19)

Jack's venting had become a nasty habit. In fact, it was wors-ening. Violence was on the horizon. The pattern had to be bro-ken. Had Jack continued down this path, it would have been right for Jill to seek the help and the discipline of Christ's church. In cases in which anger-revealers resort to violence, calling the police or other God-given authorities may be needed (Rom. 13:1–6).

A passage mentioned above, Proverbs 22:24–25, offers addi-tional counsel on dealing with those who vent their anger:

Do not make friends with a hot-tempered man, do not associ-ate with one easily angered, or you may learn his ways and get yourself ensnared. (22:24–25)

Since, as we have seen, venters beget venters, the wise per-son must avoid close contact with them. The Bible realistically recognizes the power of ungodly and godly models in our lives. We must beware of the subtle, ensnaring danger of evil asso-ciates (Prov. 1:10–19; 1 Cor. 15:33). For Jack, that meant pulling away from some of his work buddies and cultivating friendships with some mature Christian men in his church (Heb. 3:12–13; 10:24–25).

Consider one last insight from Proverbs regarding anger-revealers. Do not expect to reason with them or bring reconciliation in the midst of their rage:

> If a wise man goes to court with a fool, the fool rages and scoffs, and there is no peace. (Prov. 29:9)

In conversing with Jack about important issues, Jill learned how to "time" her comments. She understood when speaking up was wise and when it was wise to say nothing. She waited for Jack to calm down and get a grip before raising difficult topics.

PRACTICAL STRATEGIES AND STEPS FOR CHANGE

The Old and New Testament passages mentioned above furnish the truths that anger-revealers, and their counselors, need in order to change. Let's close this chapter with seven practical directives that incorporate these truths. With chapter 9, they form a counseling/self-counseling agenda.

1. *Repent of the evil desires that produce your angry behavior and receive God's forgiving, enabling grace.* As we saw in chapters 3 and 4, you must recognize and repent of the sinful beliefs and motives that cause you to reveal anger. You must uproot heart-idols and come to know the true God. Rend your hearts, not your garments (Joel 2:13). No thorough and lasting progress will be made apart from an extensive invasion of the ungodly root system. The subsequent steps assume that you have made a serious strike at the heart and that you are engaged in ongoing warfare on this level.

2. Own responsibility for your angry behavior and identify it as evil before God and man. Such anger is wicked. It is unlike God, displeasing to him, and contrary to his agenda for your life. It is also unloving and damaging to all your relationships. It brings physical and spiritual harm to those in its path and pierces those around you (Prov. 12:18). You must reject all tendencies to shift blame and accept for yourself the biblical label of a hothead. You must see the evil of your foolish ways.

Early in our marriage, my wife and I were entertaining her parents on Christmas Eve. We had planned to play the videotape of the original Christmas episode from *The Andy Griffith Show* later that evening. After supper, everyone found a seat in the living room to enjoy some Mayberry cheer.

I then remembered an important, family-related phone call that I had forgotten to make. When I mentioned—in front of everyone—my need to do this, Lauren mentioned—in front of everyone—that it would be better for me to wait, since we were all ready to watch the video. It was a good suggestion. Yet I snarled inside, then muttered a sarcastic, "A-OK, dear, whatever you say." After steaming and scheming inside for a few minutes, I realized we had a problem, and I asked to speak with her privately.

As we talked in our bedroom, my anger continued. I accused her of being bossy in front of everyone. I threatened to confront, pull rank, oppose her, etc., in front of her parents, if she ever tried that again! The tension thickened.

While we talked, however, God showed me my self-centeredness. My desire to be in control of the situation was driving me. Her family's opinion of me ruled me; the fear of man ensnared me (Prov. 29:25). (Notice the twice-repeated "in front of" phrase in my description above.) I did not want others to look at me as one of "those henpecked" husbands. They must see me as the one in charge of the evening programming.

Sadly, their approval outweighed God's approval. I valued their eyes more than God's eyes.

Furthermore, the Lord showed me how little sense I had of his presence. His keen ears heard my sarcastic words, my "reckless words [that] pierce like a sword" (Prov. 12:18). His searching eyes saw my stern face. My unloving treatment of my wife ascended to the Almighty One's throne. But I was oblivious.

What spawned my sinful behavior? It arose from an idolatrous heart. I was not resting in Christ or seeking his wisdom. The phone call could have waited another half hour. I could have planned the evening more carefully. My self-love overshadowed my love for God and my wife. Repentance meant humbling myself before God and my wife, and seeking their forgiveness.

Thankfully, we reconciled our conflict and I grew in my knowledge of both Christ and my own heart. I also learned more about how to lead and nourish my wife. We discussed how I could approach her with wisdom and sensitivity to raise concerns. In addition, the Lord gave me increasing liberty from the ensnaring fear of man. Her family's opinion of me did not matter in any ultimate way. In God's providence, this conflict became an opportunity for me to grow in Christ and glorify the Father.

3. Confess and renounce your angry behavior before God and others. Once you see your angry words and actions for what they are, you must confess and renounce them as evil (Prov. 28:13; Acts 24:16). Begin—first and always—with God (Ps. 51:4). Then go to each person whom you have offended to confess your sin, humbly seek forgiveness, and patiently reconcile the relationship (Matt. 7:3–5). This includes expressing practical steps—a game plan—through which you will pursue change.

4. Believe anew in Christ and his gospel promises to angry people. Having confessed your sins, you must receive the fresh promises that Jesus Christ gives you. You must rest in his provision of forgiving and enabling grace. Jesus died for hotheads, even for hotheads who repeatedly blow their anger. The righteous anger you deserved for your sinful anger was poured out in full fury on Jesus the Lamb. Moreover, the same grace that forgives you also empowers you as you progressively control, correct, and replace your angry behavior.

5. *Commit yourself to taking active, concrete steps to replace your angry behavior with Christlike words and actions.* Confident of God's restored favor and power, you must now pursue a specific path of change. While details go beyond the scope of this book, the thrust involves prayer, study, and practice of several key character qualities and actions:

- Self-control (Prov. 16:32; 25:28; 29:11; Gal. 5:23). This includes gentle, patient words and actions.
- Godly speech (Prov. 10:19–21, 31–32; 12:18; 15:1; Eph. 4:25–32). This includes speaking in truthful, beneficial, timely, and kind ways. Your words should edify, heal, and minister to others.
- Biblical peacemaking and problem-solving. "Blessed are the peacemakers, for they will be called sons of God" (Matt. 5:9). Your anger energy must be redirected into constructive solutions as you take proper steps to confront, forgive, and reconcile with other people. Whether you are the offender (Matt. 5:23–26) or the offended (Matt. 18:15–17; Luke 17:3–4), Jesus calls you to seek to make things right with the other person. He calls you to forgive others (Matt. 18:21–35; Eph. 4:32). You must pursue peace as a high priority (Rom. 12:18; 14:19; Eph. 4:3; 2 Tim. 2:22). Anger situations are opportunities to grow closer to your Lord.

6. *Establish and carry out a workable temptation plan.* As you begin to carry out these steps of change, you will quickly meet resistance from the world, the flesh, and the devil. You

must therefore devise and carry out a clear, workable plan to resist temptation and avoid future blowups. Such a temptation plan might include the following components:

(a) Avoid unnecessary occasions that tempt you to show anger. Temptations connected with daily duties are unavoidable and require sober watchfulness (John 17:15; 1 Cor. 5:9–10). Yet you should seek to avoid, at least at this early stage of battle, those optional places or activities that provoke blowups. Hanging out in the plant lunchroom or playing in a weeknight YMCA basketball league may be too stressful at this stage. Abstaining from contact with certain friends, associates, or neighbors may be a wise course (Prov. 22:24–25; 1:10–19; 1 Cor. 15:33).

(b) Remove yourself when possible, as quickly as possible, from explosive situations. Anger-revealers need to recognize when their frustration is mounting, and leave the scene. Family members need to give permission for, and even encourage, the person to go away to cool off. One biblical counselor actually advises "hotheads" to walk to the kitchen and stick their heads in the freezer for ten seconds!

(c) In the midst of the temptation, ask Christ for strength, and recite key verses or biblical truths you have memorized. Use 3-by-5 index cards on which you have written key passages of Scripture or concise summaries of biblical truth. Instead of counting to ten when you feel rage brewing, repeat one or two of these truths five times. Consider including one or several of the following on your cards:

- "A gentle answer turns away wrath, but a harsh word stirs up anger" (Prov. 15:1).
- "Reckless words pierce like a sword, but the tongue of the wise brings healing" (Prov. 12:18).
- "A fool gives full vent to his anger, but a wise man keeps himself under control" (Prov. 29:11).

- Truthful, Beneficial, Timely, and Kind (key words about godly speech based on Ephesians 4:25–32).
- I do not have to get angry right now. No one can make me angry. I am not a machine. Christ can help me not to blow up.
- When I blow up, I am acting like a reckless, hotheaded fool.
- When I blow up, I am like a wimpy weakling (Prov. 16:32) and an unwalled city (Prov. 25:28). I am a sitting duck for all sorts of dangers.
- What will please Jesus Christ right now? What does he want me to do this minute?

(d) Enlist mature believers to pray for you, counsel you, hold you accountable, and be available during and after crises. Godly friends and elders can serve you during this time. Select people who care, who are spiritually mature, and who will give you godly instruction—even when you would rather not hear it! Pastors and biblical counselors can guide you in this selection.

(e) Keep a log or journal of personal anger incidents. Record your situation, responses, and underlying beliefs and motives. What patterns emerge? Are there commonalities in when and with whom you vent? Writing down your sinful responses gives specific material for confession and repentance. You can also evaluate how, specifically, you need to handle such situations differently. What steps are indicated? The journal also enables your pastor, Christian friend, or biblical counselor to help you more wisely.

7. *Continue to prayerfully study Scripture, and Scripture-based resources, on relevant topics.* In the coming days, you will want to grow in your biblical understanding of anger, self-control, conflicts resolution, patience, and the tongue. Studying and memorizing the Beatitudes (Matt. 5:3–12) and the fruit of the Spirit (Gal. 5:22–23) are beneficial. Meditating on

Christ's life, especially his handling of conflicts, will pay rich dividends. Ken Sande's *The Peacemaker: A Biblical Guide to Resolving Personal Conflict* and *Peacemaking for Families,* and Wayne Mack's *Your Family, God's Way: Developing and Sustaining Relationships in the Home* make excellent supplemental reading.[3]

Thankfully, God has begun to use these steps to change Jack. While Jack has not arrived at an anger-free life, he is on the right path. His movement is visible to all, especially his family. His tirades are less frequent and less intense. He is learning to use his tongue to compliment Jill, and even to raise tough topics with her in gentle ways.

What about Jill? In our next chapter, we will examine God's agenda of change for anger-concealers.

For Further Reflection and Life Application

1. Select two or three of the verses from Proverbs that we examined, especially those that seem most forceful and memorable to you. Commit them to memory and meditate on them as you engage with people whom you find most provoking. (One way to think of meditating is to roll the verse around in the mouth of your mind like a piece of hard candy and to suck on it and savor it in stressful situations.)

2. Review the seven practical steps above. Be willing to share their content with your pastor, a mature Christian friend, or a biblical counselor, and invite him or her to help you apply this chapter's biblical counsel.

CHANGING OUR ANGRY BEHAVIOR:
SINFUL CONCEALING

You would not know at first that Jill had an anger problem. To onlookers, she seemed successful and very "together." Friends admired her ability to accomplish so much. She was a faithful wife and conscientious mother of two school-aged children. She taught Sunday school and enjoyed hosting a Bible study in her home. On top of that, Jill worked part-time in a downtown accounting office.

Yet underneath, as we saw previously, all was not well. "Inside," she admitted to her pastor, "I'm a mess." Sullen and depressed, she was a bundle of bitterness. She regularly replayed in her mind her dad's scoldings and her mom's non-involvement in her life. She daily rehearsed how her office supervisor spotted her failures but overlooked her successes. Others, too, disappointed her. Her close friend Gail seemed distant of late. Her pastor's sermons hadn't seemed very practical to her. And, of course, you remember her hotheaded husband, Jack. . . .

Jill was an angry woman, although her criticisms rarely came out in words. She had learned to conceal her anger skillfully. She clammed and internalized it. Cool and controlled on the outside, she stewed and steamed within.

Sadly, Jill is not alone. Some people cover their anger well. They manage to keep it under wraps for long periods. They master new ways to avoid people and situations that would unnerve them. Sometimes such anger-concealers resort to various escapes.

Jill enjoyed two escapes. She ran from her problems to her refrigerator. Junk food became a source of pleasure and of control amid her marital and motherly pressures. She also fled to daytime television. Soap operas furnished fantasy men who would woo and romance her. She did not crave their bodies, only the candlelight dinners and sensitive touches that Jack never gave. The talk shows engaged her mind with intriguing topics. Of course, she knew that most of the notions espoused were antithetical to a Christian worldview—at times, thankfully, the hosts even angered her. And she realized that the topics seldom applied to her life situation. Yet the conversations allowed her to forget Jack, and her job, and . . .

What does the Bible say to Jill? In our last chapter, we looked at revealed anger. Let's now consider concealed anger, the other main way in which angry behavior emerges. Like revealed anger, concealed anger offends God and ruins relationships. Sins of omission abound. Concealed anger, too, must be corrected and replaced.

What does God say about anger that goes underground, the kind that withdraws outwardly but boils inwardly? What are his answers for resentment and bitterness? How must anger-concealers change? Let's discover insights from three key passages.

THREE KEY BIBLICAL PASSAGES

Leviticus 19:16–18

Nestled in this portion of Mosaic law are relational commands reminiscent of New Testament "one another" passages.

Do not go about spreading slander among your people. Do not do anything that endangers your neighbor's life. I am the LORD. Do not hate your brother in your heart. Rebuke your neighbor frankly so you will not share in his guilt. Do not seek revenge or bear a grudge against one of your people, but love your neighbor as yourself. I am the LORD.

God's concern here is to cultivate and preserve loving relationships among his people. The passage presents specific ways in which God's people should develop and maintain oneness and guard against disunity. For example, we must not slander, hurt, or take revenge against others.

Verse 17 exhorts us, "Do not hate your brother in your heart." We saw in chapter 3 that anger begins in the heart. Leviticus 19 agrees. This passage internalizes the source of anger. Hatred starts in the heart.

The same verse offers God's alternative: to "rebuke your neighbor frankly." This Hebrew idiom is an intensive doubling of the verb that literally means to "rebuke rebukingly." True love raises the tough issues. It recognizes the exceeding sinfulness of sin, and it knows that at times nothing short of caring confrontation can free the person from its clutches. Listen to several similar calls in Scripture:

Better is open rebuke than hidden love. The kisses of an enemy may be profuse, but faithful are the wounds of a friend. (Prov. 27:5–6)

You hypocrite, first take the plank out of your own eye, and then you will see clearly to remove the speck from your brother's eye. (Matt. 7:5)

If your brother sins against you, go and show him his fault, just between the two of you. If he listens to you, you have won your brother over. (Matt. 18:15)

97

If your brother sins, rebuke him, and if he repents, forgive him. If he sins against you seven times in a day, and seven times comes back to you and says, "I repent," forgive him. (Luke 17:3b–4)

Brothers, if someone is caught in a sin, you who are spiritual should restore him gently. (Gal. 6:1a)

All this was foreign to Jill's practice. She rarely raised her concerns to the person with whom she was having conflict. She had not broached important issues with her friend Gail, her pastor, or her boss. She did not know how to, or even want to, bring up certain topics with Jack. *What if he explodes again?*

Yet Jill did carry out hidden, private rebukes. She had confronted these people in her own mind, found them guilty, and carried out her own forms of excommunication. She branded Gail as an unfaithful friend. Jill adopted a distant, complacent stance toward her pastor. Although his sermons were not very practical, at least they were not heretical. Besides, she had plenty of Christian books and radio speakers to feed her. She dismissed her boss—firing him in her mind—as insensitive and unfair. *Don't other believers have to work for unjust employers? I guess it's part of my suffering as a Christian.* Steeped in Christianized versions of "dysfunctional family" theory, she had long ago written off her "abusive" parents.

What happens when we fail to properly deal with hatred in the heart, through confrontation or forgiveness? It cooks. It stews and simmers in the heart. Revenge results and grudges develop. That is why the command to rebuke in Leviticus 19:17 is followed by the warning, "Do not seek revenge or bear a grudge against one of your people . . ." (v. 18).

Jill's responses listed above were vengeful. Her revenge was concealed, not revealed; covert, not overt. Hers were sins of omission more than commission. Her vengeance was "passive"—passive externally, but quite active in her heart.

The command "Do not . . . bear a grudge" (v. 18) translates a single Hebrew verb that means to "keep" or "harbor." Grudge-bearers keep the offender and his offense ever before their eyes, always alive in their hearts. It is precisely opposite of the way the Lord treats us, his people. The same verb describes him: "He will not always accuse, nor will he harbor his anger forever" (Ps. 103:9; cf. Jer. 3:5b; 3:12; Nah. 1:3). Unlike the wicked (e.g., Edom in Amos 1:11, same verb), God does not bear grudges against his people. Because of Jesus, he does not keep his anger against us or hold our offenses before his eyes.

This insight began to chip away at Jill. She had never grasped the cross very clearly. That God would refuse to "accuse" and "harbor his anger" against her, despite her many sins, refreshed her heart. As she began to dwell on God's grudge-free posture toward her in Christ, she saw how unlike him she had been toward others.

What must such a grudge-bearer do? He must love his neighbor as he loves himself (Lev. 19:18). This, of course, is not a command to love oneself. The Bible consistently assumes that we already do this—and far too deeply and often. Instead, the text calls us to love and serve others in the same way in which we naturally focus on ourselves (Matt. 22:36–40).

Let's glean one last insight from Leviticus. Why must we rebuke and not hate? Why must we not hold a grudge, but love the person? Verses 16 and 18 punctuate these commands with a powerful motive: "I am the LORD." Simple words, but a sobering reminder. The presence of Yahweh, Israel's covenant-keeping King and Redeemer, constrains us toward loving obedience.

The one thing that anger-concealers like Jill need most is to know the true God. We must know him as the One who no longer bears grudges against us because of Christ, and who can fill us with grace to do the same. And we must know him as the Lord who with regal authority summons and empowers us to love, not hate, and to rebuke, not take revenge.

Ephesians 4:26–27, 4:30–5:2

The apostle Paul addresses the need for whole-personed godly change in Ephesians 4:17–24. Our former way of life was a polluted pot of sinful desires, beliefs, and actions. In Christ, we must replace them with godly desires, beliefs, and actions consistent with the truth that is in Jesus and with God's purpose of re-creating us into his image.

The central arena for change to occur is in relationship with other believers. The apostle's "one another" concern is prominent in 4:25–5:2. Directives about truth-telling, working, giving, and the tongue all bear a relational import. Verses 26–27 address anger: " 'In your anger do not sin': Do not let the sun go down while you are still angry, and do not give the devil a foothold."

Human anger, says Paul, is both prevalent ("In your anger") and dangerous ("do not sin"). Believers must not "let the sun go down" on their anger. This idiom urges us to deal with anger as soon as possible and not let bitterness develop. Far too many suns and moons go down on conflicted relationships.

Sadly, Jill has let many suns and moons set without dealing with her anger, especially toward Jack and her parents. She has neither covered their sins in Christlike forgiveness nor confronted them with Christlike rebuke. She has consistently chosen the third option of keeping them before her eyes and cooking them in her heart.

What results when we fail to deal with our anger in a godly, immediate way? The devil drives a wedge into the body of Christ (v. 27). Unresolved anger and unreconciled relationships further Satan's agenda of shredding the church's unity.[1]

Jill's disappointment with her pastor, and with several other church leaders, began to affect not only her but the Bible study group meeting in her home. She found herself secretly resenting those who spoke highly of the pastor or profited from his messages. She also began to side with group members who questioned the church's status or direction. She hated the thought of being disloyal to the leaders or fanning embers of dissension. Yet she was not happy with his preaching and did not know what to do.

What does true love look like? It seeks to help others. Verse 29 urges anger-concealers to adopt a positive agenda of using the tongue to build others up, not avoid them: "Do not let any unwholesome talk come out of your mouths, but only what is helpful for building others up according to their needs, that it may benefit those who listen."

What struck Jill about this verse were her sins of omission. She had carefully avoided saying unwholesome things. She despised gossip (and gossipers), although some occasionally slipped out. Yet her dismal failure to bless people—to speak well about them and to them—became starkly clear. How seldom she had sought to help, compliment, affirm, cheer, and build up others with her words.

What shattered Jill even more was the realization that her concealed anger and sins of omission deeply offended God.

Verses 30–31 continue with this warning: "And do not grieve the Holy Spirit of God, with whom you were sealed for the day of redemption. Get rid of all bitterness, rage and anger, brawling and slander, along with every form of malice."

How, in context, do believers grieve God? On the one hand, by engaging in unwholesome speech and failing to edify others with our tongues (v. 29). On the other hand, we grieve the Spirit by our anger (v. 31).

Notice the span of anger language in verse 31. The apostle commands us to remove not only outward raging and brawling but also inward bitterness and clamming. We must replace them with Christlike kindness, compassion, forgiveness, and love for one another.

> Be kind and compassionate to one another, forgiving each other, just as in Christ God forgave you. Be imitators of God, therefore, as dearly loved children and live a life of love, just as Christ loved us and gave himself up for us as a fragrant offering and sacrifice to God. (4:32–5:2)

The apostle makes it plain that such grace toward others flows from God's kindness, forgiveness, and love toward us.

Again, as Jill pondered Christ's cross—the spotlight of God's kindness, compassion, forgiveness, and love toward her—a new view of herself and others emerged. She saw the judgmentalism she carried toward a host of people in her past and present. A new insight dawned. Her angry grudges had sprung from her unforgiving heart; this in turn had sprung from her ignorance of grace. The gospel facts and promises of Ephesians 4:32–5:2 became the new fountain from which she began to drink. These truths nourished her heart and energized her into a radical agenda of kindness, forgiveness, and love toward others.

Luke 15:25–30

Anger-concealers, as we have seen, withdraw from others and go underground with their anger. Our Lord told a sorrowful account of concealed anger in Luke 15. After the good news of the prodigal son's return and the father's joy, we read:

> Meanwhile, the older son was in the field. When he came near the house, he heard music and dancing. So he called one of the servants and asked him what was going on. "Your brother has come," he replied, "and your father has killed the fattened calf because he has him back safe and sound." The older brother became angry and refused to go in. So his father went out and pleaded with him. But he answered his father, "Look! All these

years I've been slaving for you and never disobeyed your orders. Yet you never gave me even a young goat so I could celebrate with my friends. But when this son of yours who has squandered your property with prostitutes comes home, you kill the fattened calf for him!" "My son," the father said, "you are always with me, and everything I have is yours. But we had to celebrate and be glad, because this brother of yours was dead and is alive again; he was lost and is found."

How did the older brother react to his generous father? He "became angry and refused to go in" (v. 28). He did not blow up; he simply withdrew and clammed up. The father, however, did not. He wisely approached his son to initiate conversation and draw out his thoughts. He exposed the man's resentment toward his father and jealousy toward his brother.

Jill saw this ugly trait in herself amid several relationships. Her boss was like the father and her co-worker like the younger brother. She had dutifully worked for years while this newer employee—less competent than Jill, at least in Jill's eyes—received favored treatment. Like the older brother in Luke 15, Jill withdrew and kept quiet. Outwardly she concealed her anger, but inside the coals of resentment smoldered. She needed help.

PRACTICAL STRATEGIES AND STEPS FOR CHANGE

How can you uncover your concealed anger and replace it with godly fruit? Can people really change? What directives can we offer Jill and other anger-concealers like her? The following seven guidelines, with chapter 9, form a biblical strategy for conquering concealed anger and replacing it with Christlike words and actions. At points they parallel the counsel for anger-revealers in chapter 5; in other ways they differ.

1. See the sinfulness and ugly consequences of your bitter heart and concealing behavior. As we saw in chapter 3, you

103

must identify and expose the idols in your heart, those entrenched desires and demands. While the desires themselves are not necessarily evil, they become evil when they rule your heart. Good desires easily become bad masters. Journaling helps you detect such idols and learn from anger episodes what changes are required.

Why is such anger wrong? For one thing, it grieves God by usurping his role as lawgiver, judge, and executioner (Eph. 4:30; James 4:11–12). Sinful anger is unlike our grudge-free God. It fails to reflect the cross's forgiveness to others. Such anger also produces relational distance (Luke 15:25–30) and fails to lovingly minister to others. Further, anger can injure your body. While venting harms others (Prov. 12:18), clamming harms you (Prov. 14:30). Recognizing these consequences will help fuel your repentance.

One useful homework assignment is to list specific negative consequences—in relationship to God, others, and yourself—of harboring anger. What will result if you continue to conceal your anger? Consider inviting your spouse and friends to add to your list.

Another useful project is to review the three key Scripture passages above. Then list God's acts and attributes that are in contrast to your anger-concealing tactics.

2. *Turn to Jesus Christ in repentance and faith, and believe that he fully forgives you.* Having seen the sinfulness of your anger-concealing, believe in God's provision of abundant grace in Jesus Christ. He died and rose not only for hotheads (flagrant sinners) but also for clammers (silent sinners who hide their anger). In light of his gracious promises, confess your sinful heart-idols and clamming actions and receive his forgiveness.

Furthermore, believe that there is help and hope in Christ. God's grace not only forgives but also changes sinners. One reason why many Christians make little progress in overcoming concealed anger is that they doubt God's transforming grace. He can melt your bitterness and make you a forgiver. He can teach you when to confront and when to cover over offenses, and how to do both. You need his power; thankfully, he is more than willing to give it to you. Ask him now to help you do this.

3. *Forgive your offender from your heart* (Mark 11:25). You must empty your heart of bitterness by adopting a new attitude of forgiveness. You must release the person from your judgmental grip and be prepared to reconcile the relationship.

The following six facts about nonforgivers often dislodge judgmentalism and melt bitter ice blocks. When you hold a grudge and refuse to forgive in your heart, what does God say about you?

(a) You are forgetting the size of the massive sin debt for which God forgave you (Matt. 18:21–35; Eph. 4:32; Col. 3:13).

(b) You are declaring that you do not need God's forgiveness in your life (Matt. 6:12–15; 18:21–35; Mark 11:25).

(c) You are declaring that you do not need God's mercy on the day of judgment (Mic. 6:8; Matt. 5:7; James 2:13).

(d) You are assuming God's role as Judge (Gen. 50:19; Rom. 12:19; James 4:12).

(e) You are forgetting the fact that the offender, as a sinner, is in one sense deceived and enslaved by his sin. You lack compassion (Luke 23:34a; John 8:34; Eph. 4:30–5:2; Col. 3:12–14).

(f) You are forgetting the fact that you, as a sinner, are capable of the same sin and that the same root sin may already reside in you (Prov. 16:18; Jer. 17:9; 1 Cor. 10:12; Heb. 3:12–13).

These six truths, and the accompanying passages that teach them, yield hope to those who wonder whether they can forgive

105

others. They rebuke those who refuse to forgive or to be willing to forgive. They also answer a pair of frequent objections:

- Objection: "I just can't forgive him for what he did to me." Response: "No, you can and must forgive him. God says so. And God will enable you. Jesus Christ died and rose to forgive you, call you, and empower you."
- Objection: "But you don't know how badly he hurt me." Response: "You're probably right; I don't know. But God knows. Every human on the planet has betrayed him. His Son was brutally murdered. And God is the One who declares that you can, and you must, forgive him with the same grace that forgave you. While forgiving serious offenses is neither easy nor quick, God's grace can make it happen."

While we could say much more about forgiveness, several additional assignments can benefit you, especially with the help of your pastor or a wise Christian friend:

- Study and apply the six truths. Which truths are most pertinent to you? Which are most convicting? Study and meditate on one a day for a week, and then repeat the study and meditation cycle the next week.
- Meditate on Ephesians 4:32 and Colossians 3:13, along with their contexts. Memorize and recite them daily, especially when you think about or are in proximity to the person against whom you are holding a grudge.
- Study and apply Patrick H. Morison's booklet, *Forgive! As the Lord Forgave You*.[2] Mark six key sentences and write a three- to four-sentence applicational response.
- Complete the "Pictures of God's Forgiveness of His People" in Appendix A.

4. *Resist the countertemptation to vent your anger.* Well-meaning friends occasionally advise anger-concealers to "get it off your chest," "let it out," "blow off some steam," and the like. Yet as we saw in chapter 5, such pendulum swings of discharging anger are also sinful.[3] Getting things off your chest selfishly loves *your* chest more than the chest of the person who would receive your piercing words! That's the point of Proverbs 12:18, "Reckless words pierce like a sword, but the tongue of the wise brings healing." We don't solve one sin by replacing it with another. "Do not let any unwholesome talk come out of your mouths, but only what is helpful for building others up according to their needs, that it may benefit those who listen" (Eph. 4:29). Reviewing our previous chapter will help you avoid this temptation.

Realize, instead, that there is another way to move toward others. You can learn to bless, not blast; to help, not hurt; to encourage, not injure. You must learn to . . .

5. *Replace your concealing behavior with godly speech that ministers to others.* Anger-concealers must learn to use their tongues as God-given, proactive, and intentional instruments to edify people.

The maxim "If you can't say anything nice, don't say anything at all" is sound advice, but only as far as it goes. It is a half-truth that does not go far enough. God says that you can and must *learn* to say something nice! Jesus calls you to bless even your enemies, i.e., to say good things to them and about them (Luke 6:27–46). Clamming represents a sin of omission, a serious failure to edify others (Lev. 19:17–18; Prov. 10:11, 21, 31; 12:18; Eph. 4:25, 29). Anger-concealers should study such passages and plan specific ways to speak in Christlike ways. While this is no simple task, persistent effort in dependence on God's Spirit creates new speech patterns.

Several useful personal-growth assignments can help you grow in godly speech:

- Study Proverbs 10 and 12 and write out, by hand, every verse portion that pictures edifying speech activity. After doing this, go back through and make sure that you have included Proverbs 10:11a, 13a, 20a, 21a, 31a, 32a; 12:18b, 25b. Review the list daily, meditate on the powerful images presented, and gain a vision of yourself as a nourishing speaker. Then plan specific ways to carry out this vision: "What will I say today to my spouse? When and where and how?" Log your daily successes and failures, and discuss them with a pastor, a mature Christian friend, or a biblical counselor.
- Study Ephesians 4:25–32 (perhaps with related verses from Proverbs) and write out speech guidelines based on this passage. Godly speech is truthful (v. 25), beneficial (v. 29), timely (v. 29), and kind (vv. 31–32). Memorize these four criteria, recite them daily, and prayerfully summon them to mind whenever you are tempted to withdraw. Be sure to root your grasp of these imperatives in both the gracious indicatives of Ephesians 1–3 and 4:1 and the whole-personed call to change in Ephesians 4:17–24.
- Memorize and apply "The Four Rules of Communication," based on Ephesians 4:25–32:[4]
  (a) Be honest (v. 25).
  (b) Keep current (vv. 26–27).
  (c) Attack problems, not people (vv. 29–30).
  (d) Act; don't react. Control your emotions (vv. 31–32).
- Record your successes and failures, pray for ongoing help, and discuss them with a pastor, Christian friend, or biblical counselor.
- Memorize and daily recite, pray over, and apply Ephesians 4:29.
- Read Wayne Mack's chapter on "Small Talk" in *Your Family, God's Way: Developing and Sustaining Rela-*

tionships in the Home.[5] Mark key sentences, look up the Scripture references, and write out a three- to four-sentence applicational response.

6. *Pursue biblical peacemaking and problem-solving.* People who cover their anger must unlearn their avoidance style of managing conflict and develop new skills in Christlike reconciliation. "Blessed are the peacemakers," declared our Lord, "for they will be called sons of God" (Matt. 5:9). Later in the same chapter, he laid out this agenda:

> Therefore, if you are offering your gift at the altar and there remember that your brother has something against you, leave your gift there in front of the altar. First go and be reconciled to your brother; then come and offer your gift. (Matt. 5:23–24)

Solving conflicts Christ's way requires bold commitment and consistent work. Ephesians 4:3 urges a similarly determined effort: "Make every effort to keep the unity of the Spirit through the bond of peace." The verb translated "make every effort" calls for diligent labor in keeping spiritual unity. The apostle Paul makes the same point in Romans 14:19: "Let us therefore make every effort to do what leads to peace and to mutual edification." This synonymous verb means to pursue, track down, or persecute an object. We are to seek peace aggressively. He exhorts us with the same verb in 2 Timothy 2:22: "Flee the evil desires of youth, and pursue righteousness, faith, love and peace . . . out of a pure heart." Peacemaking requires courageous expenditures of effort that exceed the natural comfort zone of concealers.

What does such conflict resolution entail? There are two godly courses you may take in the face of offense. The Christian's most frequent route should be to cover over (forgive) the sins of your offenders, as 1 Peter 4:8 enjoins: "Love covers over a multitude of sins" (cf. Prov. 10:12). In cases of more serious sin, the obedient believer lovingly confronts the offender (see quotations of Lev. 19:17–18; Prov. 27:5–6; Matt. 7:5; 18:15; Luke 17:3b–4; Gal. 6:1a listed above).

The anger-concealer, of course, chronically opts for a third path. He neither *covers* nor *confronts* offenses—he *cooks* them! He lets the person and the offense stew and steam. Instead, he must decide immediately, with God's help, to cover or confront the sins of his offenders.

Beyond studying the above Scripture texts, you will find Ken Sande's books, *The Peacemaker: A Biblical Guide to Resolving Personal Conflict* and *Peacemaking for Families: A Biblical Guide to Managing Conflict in Your Home*, to be invaluable guides to pursuing God's peacemaking paths.[6]

7. Continue to pray, to study Scripture (and Scripture-based resources), and to enlist the prayers, counsel, and accountability of fellow believers. As in all other activities of spiritual growth, thorough and lasting godly change requires constant use of God's means of grace. The truths and personal studies given in this chapter will direct your prayers. The above expositions of several key sections of Scripture, and the citations of many more, invite your further study. Each passage deserves fresh, ongoing attention.

Finally, anger-concealers need wise brothers and sisters to whom they can openly verbalize their struggles and through whom they can receive God's help (Col. 3:16; Heb. 3:12–14; 10:24–25; James 5:16). Your very soul may be at stake:

> See to it, brothers, that none of you has a sinful, unbelieving heart that turns away from the living God. But encourage one another daily, as long as it is called Today, so that none of you may be hardened by sin's deceitfulness. We have come to share in Christ if we hold firmly till the end the confidence we had at first. (Heb. 3:12–14)

Is there hope for Jill? Can she begin to get rid of her inner anger? Can she learn to forgive Jack and other sinners in her world? Can she develop new speech patterns and cultivate conflict-resolution skills?

Yes, in Jesus Christ she can, and she did! Like Jack, she has not arrived; but like Jack, she is moving along the right path. The Lord has chipped away crusty deposits of resentment. Years of bitterness have begun to break. Icy internal layers are thawing. The gospel of a grudge-free God is changing her. With new-found sweetness, Jill has begun to learn how to patiently overlook Jack's little sins and boldly confront his big ones. Jesus melts anger-concealers and makes them people who bless others.

For Further Reflection and Life Application

1. When you find yourself provoked to anger by someone who offends, consider your trilogy of options—to *cover* the person's offense, to *confront* the person about his offense, or to *cook* the person and his offense in your heart. Which do you tend to do? Why?

2. Review the seven practical steps above. Be willing to share their content with your pastor, a mature Christian friend, or a biblical counselor, and invite him or her to help you apply this chapter's biblical counsel.

7

ANGER AGAINST GOD

Carolyn was confused. Ray's affair stunned her. Matters worsened when he refused to break off the relationship. The final blow—his decision to stay with the other woman—simply shattered Carolyn's life.

Questions about Ray, the other woman, and what Carolyn should do flooded her thoughts. *What was he thinking? How could he throw away our fourteen years? Why her? How will I provide for myself? Will the divorce get ugly?*

As the initial shock gradually subsided, another, tougher crop of questions slowly emerged. *Where was God in all this? How could a good Christian like Ray turn away from what he knew to be right? Why would the Lord let the kids and me face such a nightmare? Is this what a good God does to his people?*

Carolyn was becoming angry at God, and she knew it.

What should she do about it? Was it okay to be angry with God? Several Christian friends urged her to "do the right thing" and not question God. But for Carolyn, this seemed too stoical. She felt angry! Was she supposed to simply paste on a good, Christian, plastic smile? Was she to ignore her overwhelming doubts about God's dealings? Was the radio preacher right when he said that "good Christians don't complain" in the face of trials?[1]

7

113

Other friends recommended a different path. They encouraged her to vent her feelings to God. "It's okay to be angry with God. In fact, given what you're going through, it's healthy. Don't stuff it. Tell him how you feel. Be honest; he already knows. Tell him you're angry. He'll understand. He's a big boy. He can handle it."

Carolyn was confused. The thought of expressing her anger to God made sense. It seemed so refreshing and freeing. Yet she was harboring some deep doubts about God's trustworthiness, and her conscience wasn't clear about venting so freely. To her, it felt like blasphemy.

YOUR SITUATION

Your circumstances, of course, may differ from Carolyn's. Maybe your boss fired you unfairly. Or an adult abused you as a child. Or someone you trusted betrayed you. Maybe you face financial burdens with no relief in sight, or a progressive, debilitating disease. Or maybe it's less definable. You are plodding through life with constant disappointment, a kind of pervasive inner sadness. You lack the joy that marks many Christians you know.

Whatever your specific situation, what you share with Carolyn are nagging questions about God. You mistrust his goodness. You question his wisdom. You tense up when you think of his being "in control" of your life in all its misery. In short, you, too, are angry at God.

What should you do? The good news from God's Word is that we are not left with only two options. We are not forced to choose between hiding our soul's struggles from God and venting our anger at him. The Bible rejects both in favor of a third way, a middle path that encourages transparency without endorsing blasphemy.

Let's state this way in two principles, examining each in turn.

IT IS WRONG TO BE ANGRY AT GOD

Is it okay to hold in your heart, or voice with your mouth, anger against God? No. The Bible forbids the vent-your-feelings-against-God approach.

Anger in the Bible is a whole-personed judgment that we make against a perceived wrong. We react negatively in our mind, emotions, and will against what we conclude to be evil or unfair. In this sense, anger is not merely a morally neutral emotion ("It's neither right nor wrong; it just is," as some naively argue) that exists apart from one's inner beliefs, affections, emotions, and volitions. Instead, anger is a function of our judgment. We perceive something or someone to be wrong, and we respond accordingly with our whole being.

Framed this way, the answer to our "Is it okay to be angry with God?" question is clear: No! Anger against God is wrong because it accuses God of wrongdoing. To be angry with God is to perceive some wrong in God, to apprehend some evil in his ways.

What is the root issue? Kay Arthur insightfully cuts to the core. You get angry at God, she observes, "because God did not do what you thought he should or the way he should do it or when he should do it."[2] Notice that we accuse God of not doing *what* (actions or inaction) he should do, or not doing it in the *way* (manner) he should, or not doing it *when* (timing) he should. In short, we want what we want when we want it, and when God does not deliver, we judge him.

Biblical Examples

The Bible offers numerous examples of people who were angry at God. Genesis 4 records God's rejection of Cain and his offering and his acceptance of Abel and his offering.

The LORD looked with favor on Abel and his offering, but on Cain and his offering he did not look with favor. So Cain was

115

very angry, and his face was downcast. Then the LORD said to Cain, "Why are you angry? Why is your face downcast? If you do what is right, will you not be accepted? But if you do not do what is right, sin is crouching at your door; it desires to have you, but you must master it." (Gen. 4:4b–7)

Cain wanted God to accept his sacrifice on his terms; he believed God *should* do so. When God in his holiness refused Cain's demand, Cain reacted in anger against God (along with depression, jealousy, and the murder of his brother). Cain may not have voiced this anger, but God saw it.

Was Cain's anger justified? The answer is obvious. Cain's anger at God was sinful. His sinful motives and beliefs drove his anger. He needed to repent of the sin that sought to master him and instead do what was right.

In 1 Chronicles 13, tragedy interrupted David's plan to return God's ark to Jerusalem. While the Israelites were transporting it, a leader named Uzzah "reached out his hand to steady the ark, because the oxen stumbled" (v. 9). This seemingly innocent act violated God's explicit command in Numbers 4:15 to not touch the ark. Uzzah disregarded God's holiness, and God responded with wrath. "The LORD's anger burned against Uzzah, and he struck him down because he had put his hand on the ark. So he died there before God" (v. 10).

How did King David respond to God's action? "Then David was angry because the LORD's wrath had broken out against Uzzah. . . . David was afraid of God that day . . ." (vv. 11–12). Most commentators agree that David believed that God's wrath was too harsh. David judged God to be wrong in his actions, at least in their seeming severity. Having placed God on trial, David declared God guilty.

One wonders whether David had fallen prey to the "After all I've done for you, this is the thanks I get?" mentality that often arises within us when God allows hardships into our lives. We believe that God owes us something better than the providential hardships we face. For Carolyn, it involved subtle demands that God treat her nicely because she had been a faithful wife, loving mother, and good Christian for fourteen years.

The operative clause in all such lies is this: God *should* have. . . . We can imagine David's mutterings: "Surely, God, you should have overlooked Uzzah's well-intentioned mistake." Or: "You should have punished him later, or in private, or less drastically. Your swift and harsh stroke undermined the morale of our mission—the mission we were doing for you, I might add!"

Though the narrative cites no explicit condemnation, the context implies divine disapproval of David's anger, especially in light of David's fearful decision to abort the mission. One can hardly conclude from this text that it is okay to be angry at God.

Or consider Jonah. God called his prophet to preach salvation to pagan Nineveh, the enemy of Israel. Jonah reluctantly complied. Nineveh repented, God withdrew his wrath, and Jonah became angry with God.

> When God saw what they did and how they turned from their evil ways, he had compassion and did not bring upon them the destruction he had threatened.
>
> But Jonah was greatly displeased and became angry. He prayed to the LORD, "O LORD, is this not what I said when I was still at home? That is why I was so quick to flee to Tarshish. I knew that you are a gracious and compassionate God, slow to anger and abounding in love, a God who relents from sending calamity. Now, O LORD, take away my life, for it is better for me to die than to live."
>
> But the LORD replied, "Have you any right to be angry?"
>
> Jonah went out and sat down at a place east of the city. There he made himself a shelter, sat in its shade and waited to see what would happen to the city. Then the LORD God provided

a vine and made it grow up over Jonah to give shade for his head to ease his discomfort, and Jonah was very happy about the vine. But at dawn the next day God provided a worm, which chewed the vine so that it withered. When the sun rose, God provided a scorching east wind, and the sun blazed on Jonah's head so that he grew faint. He wanted to die, and said, "It would be better for me to die than to live."

But God said to Jonah, "Do you have a right to be angry about the vine?"

"I do," he said. "I am angry enough to die."

But the LORD said, "You have been concerned about this vine, though you did not tend it or make it grow. It sprang up overnight and died overnight. But Nineveh has more than a hundred and twenty thousand people who cannot tell their right hand from their left, and many cattle as well. Should I not be concerned about that great city?" (Jonah 3:10–4:11)

What produced Jonah's anger? His evil heart. He craved the destruction of his enemies more than the glory that God would gain through their conversion. Jonah did not love his neighbor as himself. Neither love for his enemies nor compassion for the needy ruled him. Jonah believed that God had not acted the way the God of Israel should have acted.

What was God's attitude toward Jonah's anger? God disapproved. He undercut Jonah's supposed "right" to be angry. Jonah's outburst was the venting of his sinful flesh, and God exposed it as such. It was not okay for Jonah—or anyone else—to be angry at God.

We could cite other biblical examples of anger against God: the rebel kings of Psalm 2, Job's wife in Job 2, King Asa in 2 Chronicles 16 (against God's prophet), and the Jewish crowd against Jesus in John 7:23. Each reveals the same themes. Anger against God is always wrong in that it accuses God of evil.

Accusations against God

John Calvin's pastoral insights into this matter remain unsurpassed. In his sermon from Job 1:22 ("In all this, Job did not sin by charging God with wrongdoing"), Calvin asks:

> Why is it that men fret so when God sends them things entirely contrary to their desire, except that they do not acknowledge that God does everything by reason and that he has just cause? For if we had well-imprinted on our *hearts* "All that God does is founded in good reason" it is certain that we would be ashamed to chafe so against him when, I say, we know that he has *just* occasion to dispose thus of things, as we see. Now, therefore, it is especially said that Job attributed to God nothing without reason, that is to say, that *he did not imagine that God did anything which was not just and equitable.*[3]

Here lies the root problem beneath our anger against God. We accuse him of injustice. Calvin continues:

> As soon as God does not send what *we have desired*, we dispute against him, we bring suit, not that we appear to do this, but our manner shows that this is nevertheless our intent. We consider every blow, "And why has thus happened?" But from what spirit is this pronounced? From a *poisoned heart*, as if we said, "The thing *should have been otherwise, I see no reason for this.*" Meanwhile God will be *condemned* among us. This is how men exasperate themselves. And in this what do they do? It is as if they *accused* God of being a tyrant or a hair-brain who asked only to put everything in confusion. Such horrible *blasphemy* blows out of the mouths of men.[4]

Is it okay to be angry at God? No. It is to call God a "hair-brain" and to voice "horrible blasphemy." How should we counter this tendency? Calvin concludes:

119

However, the Holy Spirit wished to tell us that, if we wish to render glory to God and to bless his name properly, *we must be persuaded that God does nothing without reason.* So then, let us not attribute to him either cruelty or ignorance, as if he did things in spite and unadvisedly, but let us acknowledge that he proceeds in everything with admirable justice, with goodness and infinite wisdom, so that *there is only entire uprightness or equity in all that he does.* [5]

The solution to sinful anger at God lies in continually repenting of our remaining unbelief and rebellion. We must reject the lies that deny God's goodness, power, and wisdom, and we must reaffirm his righteousness, love, and justice. We must repent, knowing that "God opposes the proud, but gives grace to the humble" (James 4:6).

While Carolyn never read Calvin and might have winced at the thought of calling God a "hair-brain," these same truths needed to penetrate her heart. As she studied the passages of Scripture listed above, she began to see that the root of her anger with God was her subtle accusations against him: *God should not let this nightmare happen to me and good Christian families like mine.*

God's Sovereign Purposes

Before turning to our second principle—the one that guided Carolyn toward God in a positive direction—let's consider a common variation of the first principle. As a mature Christian, Carolyn knew up front that God was involved in her trial situation; this was what prompted her questions about his actions.

Don, however, did not blame God for any of his problems, at least not initially. Don was quick to blame his misery on his job—a demanding boss, unscrupulous competitors, and disloyal clients—and on his lower back injury, and the physical and financial problems it brought. He was chronically angry at others and "just upset at life overall."

In one sense, Don was committed to the Lord. He was regularly involved in worship and sought to pray and read Scripture several times a week. That is why he protested his pastor's suggestion that he was angry at God without realizing it.

Like many other Christians in our generation, Don failed to see God's sovereign hand behind his life's hardships. Yet, as Don came to realize, his problems were not random occurrences of blind chance. They came to him as the providential dealings of the omnipotent Ruler who "does whatever pleases him" (Ps. 115:3). Don had not seen that God is the ultimate cause of every hardship and that he uses every trial for the good purpose of making us like Jesus Christ (Gen. 50:20; Job 1–2; 38–42; Rom. 8:28–29).

The first turning point for Don came when he saw that God, in his sovereignty, had placed Don precisely where he wanted him to be. Yet this produced a whole new problem for Don. Before, he had been angry at "life," at "other people," at "nature," and at "the world" in general. As long as the Lord was marginal in Don's mind, Don had never blamed him for his hardships. But when God became central—when Don granted God his rightful place in the middle of his life struggles—he became angry at God. He began hauling the Lord into court.

Was this progress for Don? Actually, yes! This was the first and necessary step in a process toward deeper, more lasting joy. To move from ignorance to an awareness of God's sovereignty signals progress. The next step came as Don studied God's good purposes in sending such trials. Like Carolyn and countless other saints, Don saw that the sovereign God who stood behind his thorn-infested job and injured back was also his loving Father. He gradually saw from Scripture that the Lord was using these trials to make him more like Jesus, to draw him closer to himself, to expose his own remaining sin, to taste something of what his Savior suffered, to equip him for compassionate ministry toward others, and even to increase his longing for Christ's return and the new body and new earth promised by Christ. As Don reflected on these and similar truths, his anger at God gave way to trust in God. Don was learning to repent of his demands that God act a certain way. He was learning to love God for using these hardships for gracious purposes.

IT IS RIGHT TO EXPRESS YOUR QUESTIONS TO GOD WITH A HEART OF FAITH

If anger against God is sin, how do we deal with our doubts and questions about his providential dealings, especially amid our sufferings? Must we stoically, silently "stuff" our struggles? Thankfully, our Lord presents another option, the path laid out for us through the lament portions of Scripture.

Christians are sometimes baffled by God's ways and confused by his apparent inconsistencies. Yet Scripture teaches us the art of holy lamenting—learning how to complain in faith—to God about the calamities he sends.

For example, the careful reader of Job 1 and 2 cannot avoid the conclusion that God himself is the ultimate cause of Job's misfortune. In the chapters that follow, we hear Job's bitter complaints and heart-wrenching questions. Yet he never crossed over into a settled state of blaming God for his suffering. While Job's questions were never answered, he remained at heart faithful to God. The Lord he came to know in bolder, overwhelming ways in Job 42 was the same Lord he had trusted from the beginning.

We see the same thing in Jeremiah's book of Lamentations. He winces when he recalls God's hand of judgment on his own nation. He attributes the devastation to God's decrees, yet he never denies God's covenant loyalty or essential goodness to his people. He does not impugn God's motives or accuse him of malice or capriciousness. He wrestles, he wonders, and he questions, but he ultimately rests in God's promises of restoration and blessing.

Consider also the prophet Habakkuk on the eve of the Babylonian invasion (c. 600 B.C.). His honest complaints (Hab. 1:1–4; 1:12–2:1) arise not from anger against God but from the conviction that God was indeed a powerful Judge and a loving Savior (3:18–19). His questions reflect his fundamental faith.

Of course, the richest deposit of biblical lament lies in the psalms. Listen to David's cries in Psalm 13:

> How long, O LORD? Will you forget me forever?
>   How long will you hide your face from me?
> How long must I wrestle with my thoughts
>   and every day have sorrow in my heart?
> How long will my enemy triumph over me?
> Look on me and answer, O LORD my God.
>   Give light to my eyes, or I will sleep in death;
> my enemy will say, "I have overcome him,"
>   and my foes will rejoice when I fall.
> But I trust in your unfailing love;
>   my heart rejoices in your salvation.
> I will sing to the LORD,
>   for he has been good to me.

David grapples with God's apparent distance from him in the midst of enemy attacks. He questions the Lord's seeming neglect and complains about God's felt absence. Yet notice that David speaks *to* his God. He has dealings *with* God. He addresses God *directly*. And instead of accusing God of wrongdoing, David's fourfold "how long" lamentation (vv. 1–2) leads to petition (vv. 3–4), which yields confession of trust (v. 5) and commitment to praise (v. 6). He resolves to trust in God's loyal love, salvation, and goodness.

Laments of Faith

What common elements can we glean from these biblical laments?

1. *Suffering.* Each of these believers was experiencing intense confusion and bewilderment over apparent inconsistencies between God's revealed character and his current providential dealings. Carolyn's divorce was no less tragic than the sufferings these believers faced. Don's work and back problems were comparable to the trials recorded in Scripture. The Bible gives words to our suffering by recording the words of other sufferers.

2. *Prayer.* Each lamenter voiced his questions directly to God himself. They moved *toward* God, not *away* from him. They sought his face in prayer and settled for nothing less than conversational contact with their Savior. Job, Jeremiah, David, and Habakkuk all had direct dealings *with* God. One of Carolyn's problems was that she was asking questions *about* God but not bringing those questions to him.

3. *Faith.* The laments of these believers arose from fundamental (albeit imperfect) faith. In the trenches they submitted to God and clung to basic truths about his person and work. In fact, it was their belief in God's absolute sovereignty, power, wisdom, and goodness that produced their complaints in the first place! The mind-set goes like this:

> Father, it is precisely *because* I know that you are all-loving and all-powerful that I am struggling with the seeming absence of your love and power right now in this situation. It is *because* I am convinced that you are good that your chastisements confuse me. It is *because* I believe in your covenant love that your apparent distance baffles me.

4. *Humility.* These believers expressed their laments with reverence and submission. They didn't vent or lose control. By humbling themselves, they avoided the blasphemous accusations found in pagan religious literature.

5. *Renewal.* These saints reached some resolution of their struggle, a measure of renewal in their faith. The closing sections of Job, Lamentations, Habakkuk, and Psalm 13 all echo a mature faith, tried and tested, riper and sweeter through the hardship.

GOD'S AGENDA IN SUFFERING

Alex, a committed Christian worker, faced problems of depression and withdrawal that were tied to nightmares and memories of a childhood rape by several older boys. His struggles seriously affected his marriage and ministry. After three months of therapy that was not biblically driven and that yielded few results, he sought the help of a Christ-centered, biblical counselor.

At the root level, Alex doubted God's goodness because of this abuse. The "anger at God" question nagged him. The previous counselor had given him a book that pushed an "It's okay to be angry with God" agenda. The author urged Alex to let out his anger, and even to forgive God. Fortunately, Alex didn't buy into this approach; his biblical instincts raised red flags.

What was wrong? Like many of us, Alex had mistakenly interpreted God's heart based on his interpretation of God's providence. As his new counselor helped him look at his life through a biblical lens, Alex gained a more accurate view of his heavenly Father.

Viewing the rape incident under the biblical category of trials opened a new vista of insight and hope for Alex. He saw some of God's purposes for this trial through studying James 1:1–12, 2 Corinthians 1, Job, and the life of Joseph in Genesis 37–50.

Using Psalm 77—a lament psalm—as a model, Alex composed his own prayer of lament in which he honestly voiced his struggles. On the one hand, his growing grasp of God's goodness and grace kept him from accusing God of wrongdoing. On the other hand, he could raise the hard questions typical of biblical lamentations: "Where were you, God, when this happened? And how did you feel? Could you show me how you responded?"

These questions propelled the counseling agenda for several sessions. Alex began to see that the Lord had been on site in his life all along. Although he had not been a Christian when victimized, Alex became assured by the truth of God's electing grace that even then he had been in God's mind. His counselor helped Alex to see God's righteous anger against the perpetrators and God's promise to judge such evil (Rom. 12:19). Studying the compassion of God helped Alex see how God compassionately wept for the abuse he had suffered. God had good purposes in permitting such a horrible trial.

What gracious purposes did Alex identify? He saw that God's agenda was to lead him, as a boy then and a man now, to call on Christ and seek his help. God intended this tragedy to teach Alex to trust in God and not in himself. Furthermore, God was using this painful experience to cultivate greater compassion for fellow-sufferers (in whatever form of suffering) and to equip Alex for wiser, gentler, and more fruitful ministry to others. Today he is a merciful minister of Jesus.

NOT ANGER BUT HUMBLE, SUBMISSIVE PRAYER

What should you do when you are tempted to blame God for your suffering? How should you counsel those who are angry at him? How can you steer a middle course between stoic denial and fleshly venting?

First, reaffirm your belief in God's sovereignty, power, wisdom, and goodness toward you in Christ. Begin by meditating on the passages listed above and talking to God in prayer about what his Word is teaching you. Supplement your Scripture reading with biblically sound books on learning to trust God amid suffering.[6]

Second, reject the blasphemous temptation to accuse God of evil or cast aspersions on his character or purposes. Spurn the "It's okay to be angry at God" therapeutic voices of our day.

Third, recognize your limited ability to fathom God's decrees. Your finite, fallen mind is simply incapable of comprehending his ways. You are not responsible for figuring out God—only for knowing, trusting, and pleasing him. Resist the demand to know God's secret things, and instead rest in God's revealed things (Deut. 29:29), what his Word tells you about his loving purposes. Confess to him your ignorance of his hidden ways and affirm your essential, albeit weak or confused, faith in his goodness. Remember the cross as the final proof that God loves you (Rom. 5:8) and that he is for you amid your sufferings (Rom. 8:28–39).

Fourth, learn to acknowledge to God, in honest faith and submission, your thoughts and feelings. Be transparent in his presence; "pour out your hearts to him" (Ps. 62:8). Express your thoughts and feelings, your doubts and questions, your joys and sorrows, your groans and sighs. Yet do so with reverence. Confess to the Lord any anger you might be holding against him. Don't vent it; repent of it!

Fifth, as you learn to bring your thoughts and feelings in line with God's good purposes, be careful to obey him. Do what God commands even when it differs from your desires.

Notice Carolyn's renewed perspective: "Heavenly Father, I hate what Ray has done. It hurts. And there are times when, for the life of me, I don't know why you let this happen to the kids and me. I know you are in control, but it's hard to see your hand in all this mess, and I am tempted to get angry with you. Help me, Lord. I know deep down that you are good, that you love me and are using this to make me like Jesus. Help me to trust you and not doubt you. And help me to do what pleases you in this situation, even when I'm upset."

When tempted to be angry at God, we need not settle for cold stoicism or hot blasphemy. God opens the door for us to lament, to bring him our doubts and questions—wisely, humbly, and honestly. He inclines his ear to his suffering people. May the Lord spur us to renewed faith, holiness, and humility as we walk with him.

For Further Reflection and Life Application

1. When tempted to become angry at God, ask yourself which attribute of God you are tempted to doubt—his sovereignty, wisdom, or love—or all or some combination of these. Then ask God to renew and refresh your faith in him—in his character, absolute control, and promises.

2. Compose your own lament psalm according to the pattern described above and seen in such examples as Psalm 13 and other "How long, O LORD" types of psalms (6:3; 35:17; 74:10; 79:5; 80:4; 82:2; 89:46; 94:3; 119:84).

3. The body of Christ needs the perspectives in these chapters. Look for opportunities in the coming weeks to testify to others, in wise and sensitive ways, not only how God has been helping you repent of your anger against him but also how God has been inviting you to pour out your heart to him in humble, submissive trust.

ANGER AGAINST YOURSELF

can't believe I missed that foul shot; it would have tied the game and sent it into overtime. It's my fault we lost."

"I don't know why on earth I sold that stock; it split two months ago and continues to have a record high rise even as we speak."

"I could kick myself for burning the London broil; I would have to blow it on the very night we were hosting Jim's boss."

"To think that I threw away my marriage with Susan just for a weekend fling. I can't even look at myself in the mirror."

"What was I thinking when I dropped out my senior year to grab that high-paying sales job that evaporated in eight months? What was I thinking?"

And, as a closing commercial for you baby-boomer TV fans, "I can't believe I ate the whole thing. . . ."[1]

Mention the word "anger" and you will immediately think of some object—a person or situation or thing—against which someone's anger burns. People have anger against someone or something.

But anger is no less anger when you direct it against yourself.

Consider our working definition from chapter 1: Anger is our whole-personed active response of negative moral judgment against perceived evil. When we get mad at ourselves over some failure, we actively direct our anger inward. Our response is a negative whole-personed response, from the heart, against something we did or failed to do. Here Richard Baxter's definition of "anger" from chapter 1 can be applied well to self-anger. It is "the rising up in the heart in passionate displacency against an apprehended evil, which would cross or hinder us of some desired good."[2] Whether it's a chance to play overtime, the possession of a rising stock, an unburned beef roast, a second chance at your marriage, a high school diploma, or a night without heartburn, the person is angry at himself because his action has crossed or hindered him of some desired good. Anger comes when circumstances or people—including ourselves—thwart our lusts.

How should we think about this very real notion of being angry at self? It's remarkably similar to the notion of "self-forgiveness." In both cases, I make a moral judgment that my action or inaction is wrong—not necessarily a violation of God's law, but robbing me of something I now want. I judge myself to have done something wrong and now wish to punish myself. Self-anger describes my wrath against myself; the unbiblical notion of self-forgiveness posits my need to forgive myself of my sin and release my anger.

Both self-anger and self-forgiveness are in turn similar to the dynamics of shame or regret. In the latter I perceive that my action or inaction is wrong in the sight of others; I am embarrassed before other people's eyes because of my failure.

How should we think biblically about being angry at self? As we saw in chapter 1, the Bible speaks of divine anger, righteous human anger, and sinful human anger, but it doesn't picture that anger being directed against self. At the same time, the Scripture does speak of the condemning power of one's conscience in passages such as Romans 14:22–23, 1 Corinthians 4:2–4, and 1 John 3:19–21.

130

Let me suggest five ways in which the Bible addresses this matter of self-anger. Any or all of them may underlie a person's experience of being angry at himself.

1. The person who is angry with himself may simply be expressing his inability or unwillingness to grasp and receive God's forgiveness.

This explanation especially fits the person who has actually and unambiguously—in fact, not in mere perception—sinned against God. Such a person sees his self-anger as a punishment for the guilt that his action or inaction has incurred. I'm mad at me because, while my conscience tells me I deserve punishment, in my unbelief I do not see God's judgment and forgiveness concurrently poured out on me.

Why might a Christian not grasp God's forgiveness? Perhaps he has failed to see his sin as a direct and serious offense against God himself (Gen. 39:9; Ps. 51:3–4). His conscience is not quiet because he has underestimated the seriousness of sin. He rationalizes it as a mere mistake, not a treacherous assault against his Creator and King. Hence, he is not driven to seek God's grace for his sins; instead, he chews over his mistakes with gnawing, undefined regret.

In a similar way, maybe he has failed to see and appreciate God's holiness and wrath against his sin (Isa. 6:5). His conscience tells him that his sin must be judged and punished. If God won't do it, or God's wrath is regarded as too light, the angry man will supply the needed anger. Because he underestimates God's hatred of sin, he believes he must judge it himself and be angry about it. The real God is simply not in the picture.

Perhaps the person has not gripped the scope and depth of God's forgiving grace and power (1 Cor. 6:9–11; Phil. 3:13–14; 1 Tim. 1:15–16). He disbelieves the truth that God can forgive even the worst of sinners. With such a narrow, limited God, he sees his sin as unforgivable and in need of his own punishment. Or he views God's grace as "cheap," not powerful enough to break the hold of sin.

Maybe the person struggles with forgiveness because he is not properly responding to the obstacles that hinder assurance and tempt him to doubt. These can include Satan the accuser (Zech. 3:1; Rev. 12:10), human accusers, the lingering remnants of the same sin, or the ongoing reminders of past sin (places, relationships, physical scars). When he succumbs to such temptations, he may be filled with angry regret and wrongly think he needs additional self-forgiveness.

Perhaps he has failed to grow in the graces of putting off the particular sin and putting on righteous replacements (Eph. 4:22–24). He doubts God's forgiveness because he repeats the same sin. And he repeats the same sin because, in terms of growth, he is the same person. His stunted sanctification results in repeated defeat at the hands of this besetting sin. And his ongoing "inability to forgive himself" is a veiled surrender to its binding power. He is mad at himself for his ongoing sin.

The remedy in all such cases is to properly understand, believe, and live out the gospel. Holding onto God's forgiveness in Christ undercuts all these errors and removes the risk of misunderstanding our true problem (i.e., a need for deliverance from sin's guilt and power) as anger against self. What we really need is to turn from our unbelief to the true gospel of grace!

Phil, the man who threw away his marriage for a weekend tryst with another woman, desperately needed to understand God's gospel grace. The relationship began as an innocent friendship but developed a life of its own, culminating in adultery. "I can't believe how stupid I really was," Phil told his friend and church elder. "I've wrecked my marriage completely; Susan will never give me a second chance." Despite his efforts to repent and seek forgiveness from both God and his wife, his anger against himself continued. His disgust as he looked at himself in the mirror was more than the proper guilt and shame that his infidelity warranted. Not seeing a God who judged him and a Savior who died for him, Phil had only himself to deliver the needed punishment of self-anger. And there he wallowed in his guilt, groping for self-atonement through penance and mental self-laceration. And every reminder of his wife, their marriage, their house, and their children only magnified his raging regret. His thoughts of suicide were not driven by despair but by self-murderous desires. Phil hated the man he had become, and in a twisted way he had sentenced himself to death.

What was Phil's hope? Only the cross—the death sentence imposed and executed on his substitute, the Lord Jesus. As Phil learned of the work of Christ, he was able through repentance and faith to move past his self-anger, to entrust his guilt and his judgment to the mighty Savior of sinners.

2. The person who is angry with himself may not see or be willing to acknowledge the depth of his own sinful nature.

The person who says he is mad at himself for what he did may simply mean "I still can't believe that I—I, a good moral person, I, the great I—actually did such a dastardly thing!" Such a person fails to understand that none of us, as sinners, is above the most deceitful and desperately wicked acts (Jer. 17:9; 1 Cor. 10:6–12).

Our ability to do evil should not surprise us, once we understand the sinful nature that reigns in the unbeliever and remains in the believer. James 1:13–15 pictures the power of our corrupt desires to bring us to spiritual ruin. The Puritan theologian John Owen observed that any kind of sin carries within itself the seeds of total apostasy.[3] Your self-anger may simply be the result of naively believing that you are better than you really are.

3. The person who is angry with himself may be venting his regrets for failing to achieve a certain cherished desire.[4]

133

The boy who missed the game-tying free throw and the man who sold his stock before its rapid rise have this in common: their failures mean that they will not get the good things they treasured. In essence, such a person says this: "I had an opportunity to get something I really wanted, but I threw it all away." The basketball player moans, "I could have tied the game for my team!" The investor sulks, "I could have been rich!"

The particular ruling desire may vary: "I want to be liked by my classmates." "I want to be married." "I want to be approved by my boss." "I want to have children who respect me." "I want to see my dying dad find salvation."

But the reality then sets in: "But somehow by my sin [real or perceived], I've blown it." "I said something stupid in class in front of my peers." "I embarrassed my girlfriend [i.e., potential fiancée] in the restaurant." "I froze up in Dad's hospital room instead of speaking a good word about Jesus."

The bottom line: "And now I hate myself for squandering the opportunity to get what I had been longing for. I had happiness in the palm of my hand and dropped it!"

Do you see the lie that drives the self-angry person? He proudly thinks that he can control the world and guarantee getting what he wants. When his desires are thwarted, the result is self-reproach and a haunting case of "if only I had. . . ." He is blind to his underlying urge to control his own happiness. When he fails to reach his earthly dream, he gets mad at himself.

Do you see the similarity to the dynamics in chapters 3 and 4? There we saw that our heart-idols produce demands on others, and when they fail to give us what we crave, we get angry at them. The same is true here: We fail to get what we crave, and we get angry at ourselves.

The solution is also similar to that in the previous chapters. We must confess the deceptiveness and power of our ruling desires, and repent of their rulingness. In humble faith we meet a forgiving Savior, and in his strength we dethrone those idols and learn to rest in him. Self-anger recedes. Contentment rises. Jesus reigns.

4. The person who is angry at himself may be trying to establish or live under his own standards of righteousness.

Self-anger may simply mean that the person hasn't lived up to his own standards or to other people's expectations (which he adopts as his standards). We expect a certain level of performance from ourselves. We set unrealistic, perfectionistic goals. When we fail, as we inevitably do, we get angry at ourselves.

In essence, such a person has proudly erected his own law or fearfully embraced someone else's law. He is pursuing not only "a righteousness of [his] own" (Phil. 3:7–9) but a righteousness of his own against *standards* of his own. But the Bible tells us that God is the only one we must please; his law must be our sole standard of self-measurement. When we accept other standards, we open ourselves to self-anger when we fail.

For example, the man who gets mad at himself when he makes a job mistake has erected an unbiblical standard: "I must be a flawless worker." He is playing God by rejecting God's law and establishing his own. The woman who is upset with herself because, in her words, "If only I had persuaded my husband to go to the doctor earlier, he wouldn't have died," is likewise assuming God's role. Thankfully, the gospel is more powerful than even a distorted conscience.

As I was writing this chapter, I spoke with a couple who had endured a disappointing vocational experience. Sid had relocated to a southern state to take a middle-management job with a large company. The job seemed perfect for him, an ideal job with a solid salary and benefit package and plenty of potential for growth. What Sid had underestimated—severely—was the cutthroat corporate climate and his family's understandable displeasure with both the community and the questionable company. After nine months, he resigned and they moved back to their hometown jobless and in debt.

Sid later admitted that he had been myopic, focusing on the job more than his family and focusing on the job's allure—its perks and potential—more than its many downsides. He had been enticed by the company's come-ons. His good desires had become bad masters.

But the one who struggled even more was Jane. From Sid's initial mention of this job opportunity, to his first interview, to his family's visit to house-hunt, to the day of relocation, Jane was uneasy with the move.

As events unfolded, Jane grew increasingly angry with herself for not stopping Sid from pursuing and accepting this position. Her hindsight featured a dozen "if only" and "why didn't I?" regrets. *If only I had spoken up earlier. If only I had asked Sid or the interviewer more questions. If only I had insisted that Sid wait a week before impulsively accepting the offer.* And the most extreme of all: *If only I had packed my bags and drove myself and the kids back home for a few days to show Sid that I didn't want to be there.* Her regrets were drowning her in guilt and self-anger.

What was going on inside Jane? Among the many heart themes we discussed was the distorted guilt behind the self-anger. She was mad at herself because she wrongly believed she was responsible to get her husband to pull out of the job application–interview–acceptance path. It was not enough for her to do what she did, i.e., to clearly voice her doubts and concerns to her husband at various points. She was owning responsibility not only to communicate to him (which she did) but also to control his decision (which she did not and could not!). Her self-anger flowed from her submission to a law that was not from God.

5. The person who is angry with himself may have ascended to the throne of judgment and declared himself to be his own judge.

136

To be angry at myself is to place myself in the role of judge. I convene the court, prosecute the case, render a guilty verdict upon myself, and express my anger. But the Bible declares that God alone is Judge and that his Son alone is my penalty-bearer and forgiver.[5]

This role issue is important. What is the person actually saying when he speaks of being angry at himself? Is "he" somehow angry with his "self," or is it vice versa? Who is the "he" who judges his "self"? And who is the judge who determines that guilt even exists in the first place?

It is vital in this instance that we point the angry person away from himself as judge or forgiver to the one and only Judge and Forgiver, our Lord Jesus Christ!

We began this chapter with some typical examples of people who get angry with themselves. And we have seen five ways in which this diagnosis actually falls short by not grasping the depths of human depravity and the heights of divine grace. We must not minimize our guilt—the actual or distorted types—but take it to the cross. God's Word provides the only accurate, helpful diagnosis and solution.

What a rich ray of grace this is for self-angry sinners like us! Our experience of self-anger—e.g., self-recrimination, self-accusation, and brooding—provides a marvelous window into a deeper perception of our subtle sinfulness. We fail to see the ways in which we blindly live as our own so-called "righteous lawgiver and judge, as well as sacrifice for sins." Such deepened self-knowledge opens the door for us to know the love of God in Christ Jesus with fresh relevancy and power.

What does this mean for us? We need not hold anger against ourselves. The blood of Jesus cleanses all our unrighteousness. "Son, your sins are forgiven" (Mark 2:5). Instead of the endless drip of regret, God now showers us with his forgiveness.

His promises of daily grace cascade upon us like a vigorous waterfall.

Which promises? The following passages, with their word pictures, can became especially persuasive: "I have removed your sins as far as the east is from the west. Though they were like scarlet, I have made them white as snow. I have put all your sins behind my back. I, even I, am he who blots out your transgressions, and remembers your sins no more. I have swept away your offenses like a cloud, your sins like the morning mist. I have trod them underfoot and hurled them into the ocean depths" (Ps. 103:12; Isa. 1:18; 38:17; 43:25; 44:22; Mic. 7:19).

May God enable us to deal with our self-anger through the gospel and to help others do the same.

For Further Reflection and Life Application

1. When you find yourself angry with yourself in some prolonged or long-standing way, be it the strong "I hate myself" sort or the gnawing-regret sort, try on the five explanations above to see whether one of them fits your experience. Notice how all five ways focus on the basic issues of the gospel—sin and grace, God's judgment and Christ's redemption. Beware of simplistic, even Christian-sounding notions that people might offer to diagnose and explain your struggle, such as "You just need to forgive yourself."

2. Study the passages in Appendix A's Bible study, "Pictures of God's Forgiveness of His People." Dwell on these rich pictures of grace. See their fulfillment in the cross of our Lord. Feast on the forgiveness that God lavishes on you. Ask him to replace the self-anger in your soul with the joy of Christ's redemptive work. And share this study, and your testimony, with a friend.

9

HELPING OTHERS DEAL
WITH THEIR ANGER

There are various reasons why you may be reading this book. Maybe you're reading it for your own sake. You wish to handle your own anger better and improve your relationships with God and others.

Or maybe someone you care about has a serious anger problem. Perhaps you are eager to understand why your friend is so frequently angry and you want to offer some practical help.

But more than likely both are true. Even if you picked up this book to get some self-help, you are seeing the faces of many friends and family members on these pages. In other words, as Paul Tripp put it, you are a person in need of change who wants to help others in need of change.[1] Or maybe you're a pastor or elder or Christian counselor to whom God has given a special ministry vision and calling to help angry people grow and change in Christ. In my own case, I began studying anger to be a better pastor, to minister God's Word more skillfully to some angry people I knew. Yet in the course of my pursuit, God changed me.

Whatever your status, you are to be commended for your desire to help. God in Christ calls each of his children to minister to one another in many ways, including counseling one another with God's Word.[2] The world out there—and your own world around you—has plenty of angry people who need these Christ-centered perspectives.

In light of this, how do you minister God's truth in specific ways to angry people?[3] How can we become wiser, more gracious people-helpers as we meet angry people? Let's consider a basic three-step agenda and some tools to help angry friends and family members, whether or not they admit to having an anger problem.

Step One: Enter the Person's World, Understand Him and His Situation, and Give Gospel Hope

Your initial aims in helping an angry person are to reflect Christ's care and hope for him and to cultivate a warm, welcoming relationship. Jesus our great high priest offers mercy and power to all, including angry people, who look to him. From him we may "receive mercy and find grace to help us in our time of need" (Heb. 4:16). God's Word—the Book about anger—gives answers to anger problems.

Gaining information ("data-gathering") about the person is vital; you can't help people you don't know. In fact, your intimate knowledge about even your own friends and family members is usually far less than you realize. Most of us have very few relationships that break the surface.

You will want to start with general information and move progressively toward specifics. This means understanding and responding with Christlike interest to the person's significant past influences, present circumstances, and future concerns. What are his situational pressures? How have people sinned against him? When? By whom? In what ways? Where is he being tempted? Compassionate listening is vital.

Why are these matters so important? Because angry people are frequently defensive and mistrusting. They will not open their lives to you unless you show genuine desire to hear their stories, including their hardships. Getting "on board" with them opens the door to further opportunities to instruct and per-suade. Moreover, it is not enough that you understand them; you must communicate this to them. In other words, to gain their ears, they need to *know* you understand and that you care.

Knowing the person also requires understanding his specific anger incidents. When does he get angry? What triggers it? On what occasions? Against whom? Where, when, and how? What does he do and say in anger? What patterns does he report? Which do you suspect?

You gain this information not only by asking good questions and listening well, but also by watching your friend's non-verbal behavior and hearing the tone, inflection, and volume of his words. The friend who protests with an intense, raised voice, "No, I wasn't angry at her," needs your Christ-centered friendly intervention more than he admits. In addition, as you get to know him better, you may also begin to feel some of his anger directly. He may begin to let down his guard and let out his anger. And you may be the recipient.

Another way to get to know the person is through various homework assignments, such as the samples in Appendix A. Don't assume that you can't suggest assignments in your infor-mal counseling or discipling relationships. Like lending a neigh-bor your wheelbarrow, sharing a Christian growth tool or two with a friend who has confided in you and shown interest in Christ will only elevate your friendship and will show your friend that you are a true friend who wants to help.

For example, the "Journaling a Problem Incident" sheet invites him to assess an anger incident—to describe the situa-tion and then briefly note what he felt, said, did, thought, and wanted in that situation. Depending on the problem area and your insights from your conversations, you can tailor the home-work to ask him to focus on anger toward a specific person or in a specific situation (e.g., "write up some of the anger inci-dents you are having at work"). You will notice that the form is not limited to anger incidents but can be used to reflect on issues of conflict, anxiety, etc.

Other formats can also work. You might encourage your friend to journal in a notebook his thoughts or prayers related to anger. You can use this exercise to teach him how to distinguish between root and fruit, situation and response, sinning and being sinned against, and concerns versus responsibilities. The journal also helps you to get to know him better as he shares with you and as you enter his daily world and see life through his lens.

Throughout this first step, you must continually present the hope of Christ. Help your friend from the outset to believe that Christ forgives and changes angry people, and that God's Word has answers to his anger problems. Help him to discover these truths himself through the means of grace, both private (e.g., reading and meditating on Scripture, prayer) and public (e.g., worship, Bible teaching, service, "one another" fellowship with mature believers).

Remember, too, the powerful impact that your own example can have on others. No small part of Christlike ministry is to reflect Jesus, who is gentle, humble, and inviting to sinners (Matt. 11:28–30). Your relationship to the person sets a context for teaching wisdom (James 3:17–18), demonstrating gracious speech (Prov. 15:1; Col. 4:6), and modeling godly behavior (Prov. 13:20; 22:24–25). This ministry also includes wise disclosures of personal illustrations including both your successes and failures. Testimonies of God's transformation of your own angry heart will go a long way to give your friend hope and foster his trust in you.

As you gain understanding of your friend and as his trust in you develops, your task is to lead him from idols to Jesus. This begins in a general way from the start as you speak of Christ's grace and power, and invite hope and faith. Stressing the facts of the gospel—Christ's death and resurrection for sinners like us—and the promises of God must be your priority. Key passages for memorization and meditation that instill help and point to Christ's provisions for sinners include John 6:68–69; 1 Corinthians 10:13; Ephesians 1:3; Colossians 2:3, 9–10; Hebrews 4:16; and 2 Peter 1:3. Reading and recording insights and applications from John 1 or Ephesians 1–2 may help. Booklets such as Jay Adams's *Christ and Your Problems* and Jerry Bridges's *You Can Trust God* can supplement your use of Scripture in giving hope.[4]

Based on this grace, you then invite your friend to respond with a commitment to live for Christ, please God, and apply God's answers to his life. Key passages include 2 Corinthians 5:9, 14–15 and Ephesians 4:1, 17–31; 5:8–10. At the same time, you must make allowances for people who remain tentative at this stage. The angry person may be unconvinced that Jesus is worthy of his allegiance and that Jesus can truly forgive and change him.

Step Two: Help the Person to Root Out His Sinful Heart Beliefs and Motives that Cause Sinful Anger and to Embrace the God of Grace

As you address specific anger issues, it's vital that you help your friend see that his anger arises from his own heart. As we saw in chapter 2, people will offer half a dozen explanations for their anger that will fall short of the Bible's simple but piercing diagnosis. You, of course, must be convinced that this connection is indispensable, i.e., that thorough and lasting godly change happens only when our heart beliefs and motives are radically changed by God's grace. Reviewing chapters 3 and 4 may help you to solidify this link between heart and behavior.

The heart of your work at this stage is to expose your friend's ruling beliefs and motives, and to teach him and persuade him in fresh ways to repent and believe Christ. You might find it most helpful to ask him to read James 3:13–4:12, or one of the

Bible stories that we considered previously. The "James 4 and the Cause of Conflicts" Bible study in Appendix A can serve to lead him into the passage to discuss it with you or to follow up your meeting together.

Expect to find in your angry friend the typical idol clusters faced by you and other sinners. Maybe they clutch for control over circumstances and relationships. Parents explode when their children buck their authority. Wives angle to get their husbands to go to church. Husbands demand that their wives submit sexually. Workers build their hopes on a promotion or raise. Pastors demand members to perform well; members expect the same (and sometimes more) from their pastors.

Comfort and convenience can also rule people. A dad yells at his son for interrupting his evening affair with his newspaper. An employee complains about the boss's assigning him extra work. A pastor's wife resents the constant phone calls from a chronic complaining congregant.

Or perhaps the person's fear of man—his idols of approval and reputation—causes anger. An embarrassed husband erupts when his wife fails to clean the house before their friends arrive to visit. A defensive wife resents her husband's critical comments about her in front of his parents. The performance-driven schoolteacher collapses when her students criticize her.

What assignments help flush out specific idols? Along with the items mentioned above, the "Inventory of Personal Needs and Rights" in Appendix A addresses our so-called "unmet needs." Biblical counselors know that the items listed in the inventory are not true "needs" or "rights" in God's eyes. But gaining this data of your friend's felt needs is helpful as you teach him the biblical perspective.

During this phase, you should encourage the person to continue journaling his anger incidents. As he begins to understand his heart issues with biblical insight, the journal begins to reflect a repentant heart. The person may progressively transform it from a problem journal to a prayer journal, addressing God with second-person pronouns. John Bettler suggests a useful syllogism to help identify specific idol issues.[5] Help your friend to fill in the blanks in the following statements for each anger episode (sample answers supplied in italics):

1. "I must/must not be *inconvenienced*."
2. "Your job is to *make my life convenient*."
3. "Because you failed, you are bad and I have a right to punish you."[6]

Notice the ingredients of sinful anger:

1. "I must not be inconvenienced" = an idolatrous drive ("must") for something (convenience), even something that in and of itself is not bad.
2. "Your job is to make my life convenient" = a self-centered, unreasonable demand placed upon you to give me that idol.
3. "Because you failed, you are bad and I have a right to punish you" = a judgmental, punitive verdict on you as a transgressor.

Or consider Ken Sande's useful summary of the progression of an idol, found in his *The Peacemaker* and *Peacemaking for Families*.[7] We start with a legitimate "I desire," but that too often becomes a sinful "I demand." When another person fails to satisfy my demands (and let's note that no one can!), I develop an internal "I judge" posture, which then gives rise to an "I punish" agenda. While Sande's topic is conflict, the application to anger is obvious and direct. His application questions also found in both these works can also serve as heart-revealing homework assignments.[8]

Of course, it is not enough to help the person uproot idols. You must help him replace his false trust with renewed trust in the living God and with a growing confidence in his resources centered in Christ and in his Spirit, his Word, and his church.

While every act, attribute, and promise of God will increase the believer's faith, three truths seem particularly vital for those with angry hearts:

1. God Is the Righteous Judge of Your Offenders. Angry people who have been sinned against, sometimes severely, need to know that a just God will punish sin and vindicate his people. They need to let God be angry for them, to let the Lord be their sole lawgiver, offense-recorder, witness, prosecutor, judge, and executioner. Urge your sinned-against friend to trust in God's perfect justice—perfect in discernment, in timing, and in degree of punishment. In his own time and his own way, he will condemn the guilty and vindicate the righteous.

What does this sound like? "Dear friend, I know that So-and-So has hurt you deeply, but God sees. He is just. Leave room for his wrath. Let God be God. Let him be angry for you. Refuse to play vigilante. Let him defend you before your accusers and prosecute your enemies, in his time and in his way. Besides, he can do a much more thorough job than you ever will. He alone can sort out the wheat and the tares. Don't get in his way."

Key passages to teach or assign include Psalm 94; Romans 12:14–21; 13:1–7; 2 Thessalonians 1:6–8; 1 Peter 2:22–23; 4:19; Revelation 6:9–11. Jay Adams's *How to Overcome Evil: A Practical Exposition of Romans 12:14–21*[9] has helped many Christians fight this battle. Encourage your friend to read the book, mark key sentences, record insights and applications, and talk with you about them next week.

2. God Is the Merciful Forgiver and Righteous Judge of Your Sins. Angry people focus on the specks in others' eyes and ignore the planks in their own (Matt. 7:3–5). The place to begin to dislodge this self-centered distortion is to know that for believers, God in Christ has forgiven their massive, multi-

146

million-dollar sin debt against him. Key passages for the person to study include Psalms 32; 51; 103; 130; Isaiah 38:17; 43:25; 44:22; Jeremiah 31; Micah 7:18–20; Matthew 18:21–35; Ephesians 4:32; and Colossians 3:13.

One specific assignment is to study, record, and meditate on the rich word pictures of divine forgiveness in the Psalms, Isaiah, Jeremiah, and Micah passages listed above (see Appendix A, "Pictures of God's Forgiveness of His People"). Such a study also prepares your friend for God's call to forgive those who have sinned against him. Jerry Bridges's book *Transforming Grace* and Patrick Morison's booklet *Forgive! As the Lord Forgave You* will teach the same truths.[10]

In addition, we want to help angry people expand their awareness of and reverence for God as their holy Judge. While tempted to return evil for evil, they need to know that God's holy eyes gaze upon them. "The fear of the LORD is the beginning of wisdom" (Prov. 9:10); such reverent wisdom is required when facing mistreatment. The apostle Peter appealed this way to suffering Christians: "Since you call on a Father who judges each man's work impartially, live your lives as strangers here in reverent fear" (1 Peter 1:17; cf. 2 Cor. 5:9–10).

3. God Is Your Good, Loving, and Sovereign Father. Angry Christians often feel out of control—lost, abandoned, and orphaned in a world out of control. Our agenda is simple: help them know God as their Father. They are sons, not slaves; heirs, not orphans (Gal. 3–4). Direct your friend to list and meditate on God's attributes in passages such as Genesis 37–50 (especially 50:19–20); Matthew 6:19–34; Luke 12:22–32; and Romans 8:28–39.

Again, there are excellent Christ-centered books to aid us. Suggest to your friend Jerry Bridges's book, *Trusting God: Even When Life Hurts*, his abridged booklet, *You Can Trust God*, or John J. Murray's *Behind a Frowning Providence*.[11] Bridges presents a memorable triad of truths about God that I often draw for people and call the "Trusting God Triangle": God is . . .

- Sovereign and all-powerful;
- Infinitely wise and working according to his plan; and
- Perfectly loving and good toward his people.

These facts can bring renewed hope to your struggling friend or family member.

Before moving to our third phase of ministry, let's remember our goal at this point. Having cultivated a relationship with the person, you are seeking to help him uproot his sinful anger by dislodging his ruling desires and shifting his faith to the living God. The triune God is using you to expose and change your friend's sinful beliefs and motives. He opposes the proud, but gives grace to the humble (Luke 12:32; 18:9–14; Heb. 4:16; James 4:6). It is vital that you deal thoroughly with these heart issues.

Step Three: Help the Person to Control His Sinful Anger Expressions and to Replace Them with Godly Words and Actions

Having led your friend to embrace the God of grace, in this phase you seek to help him change his angry behavior. The direction you take depends on the type of anger he expresses. You must tailor the biblical call to control and replace sinful words and actions to fit the particular person.

When dealing with anger-revealers like Jack, recall our chapter 5 guidelines:

1. Repent of the evil desires that produce your angry behavior and receive God's forgiving, enabling grace.
2. Own responsibility for your angry behavior and identify it as evil before God and man.
3. Confess and renounce your angry behavior before God and others.

148

4. Believe anew in Christ and his gospel promises to angry people.
5. Commit yourself to taking active, concrete steps to replace your angry behavior with Christlike words and actions:
   - Self-control.
   - Godly speech.
   - Biblical peacemaking and problem-solving.
6. Establish and carry out a workable temptation plan. This includes enlisting the help of fellow believers.
7. Continue to prayerfully study Scripture, and Scripture-based resources, on relevant topics.

Along with these guidelines, we considered a host of biblical passages for anger-revealers. In your personal ministry, you can tailor these texts into various creative assignments. One tool to use in Appendix A is a study from Proverbs entitled "Controlling Your Angry Behavior." Encourage the person to complete it and then discuss it with you afterward, and to adopt one or two of the verses as sharp arrows to attack sinful anger. Several of them, especially Proverbs 12:18 and 29:11, serve as excellent memory verses.

How do we help anger-concealers like Jill? Chapter 6 examined the sinful ways in which people conceal, internalize, and clam their anger. Scriptures such as Leviticus 19:16–18, Luke 15:25–30, and Ephesians 4:25–5:2 can help your friends see the evil of such behavior. Recall the following guidelines:

1. See the sinfulness and ugly consequences of your bitter heart and concealing behavior.
2. Turn to Jesus Christ in repentance and faith, and believe that he fully forgives you.
3. Forgive your offender from your heart.
4. Resist the countertemptation to vent your anger.

5. Replace your concealing behavior with godly speech that ministers to others.
6. Pursue biblical peacemaking and problem-solving.
7. Continue to pray, to study Scripture (and Scripture-based resources), and to enlist the prayers, counsel, and accountability of fellow believers.

The third guideline, "Forgive your offender from your heart," requires special attention. We must help our friends release bitterness and forgive the offender attitudinally, from the heart. Books such as Ken Sande's *The Peacemaker*, Jay E. Adams's *From Forgiven to Forgiving*,[12] Patrick Morison's *Forgive! As the Lord Forgave You,* and Paul David Tripp's *War of Words*[13] can guide counselors and counselees through the intricacies of forgiveness, including the distinctions between attitudinal/heart forgiveness and transactional/granted forgiveness.

One helpful Bible study/teaching tool in Appendix A is "Battling Bitterness with the Gospel," coupled with the truths about forgiveness in chapter 6.

Chapters 4 and 5 suggested other homework assignments. In addition, you can use Wayne Mack's manuals that contain various practical homework materials, including self-analysis, biblical teaching, practical suggestions, and Bible studies.[14]

One further clarification: The Bible teaches that these behavioral changes will honor God and reflect thorough and lasting godly change only *if* they flow from the kind of heart repentance we envisioned above. But this does not mean that in our personal ministry we should fail to consistently call for such obedience from the onset of our ministry. In fact, our very insistence on obedience and self-control from the start will often expose the person's need for grace and create dependency on God. In other words, by exhorting anger-revealers to cease their venting immediately and urging anger-concealers to speak in honest, edifying ways now, you actually drive them *to* Christ and the gospel. In my own case, I can see that the same Bible that opposed my angry expressions also exposed and hacked my angry roots and pointed me to the Redeemer, in whom judgmental demanders like me find forgiving mercy and life-changing grace.

Helping angry people can be costly—it will cost you your time to cultivate a relationship with and talk with your friend. It will cost you the energy of reading your Bible and praying. And it may even subject you to the other person's anger. But the riches of serving our Lord in this ministry far outweigh our investment. To see friends, family members, and fellow church members humbling themselves before the God of grace is a rich reward, as James 5:19–20 reminds us:

> My brothers, if one of you should wander from the truth and someone should bring him back, remember this: Whoever turns a sinner from the error of his way will save him from death and cover over a multitude of sins.

For Further Reflection and Life Application

1. Meditate on the following passages (referred to above; see note 2): Romans 15:14; Galatians 6:1–2; Ephesians 4:12–16; Colossians 3:16; 1 Thessalonians 5:12–13; Hebrews 13:12–13; James 5:19–20. Ask God what kind of personal ministry he would want you to have in the lives of your friends, especially those who are angry.

2. List two or three friends, fellow church members, or family members who might be struggling with anger. Review the three ministry strategy steps in this chapter and plan some specific steps to begin to enter the world of one of these persons to cultivate a wise, caring ministry relationship. Enlist the prayer support and guidance of a pastor or a mature Christian friend as you prepare to minister in this way.

151

3. As you minister to people, realize that your desires for them to grow and change can easily become a demand, and that anger toward them can quickly develop. As you move forward in ministry, be prepared for ways in which you will be tempted and be quick to practice what you preach.

WHY YOU MUST DEAL WITH YOUR SINFUL ANGER

Knowing and doing are not the same thing. If you have followed our path through the previous nine chapters, then you have learned a lot about anger:

- You now view anger not as a thing or merely as an emotion but as a whole-personed negative reaction of moral judgment against a perceived wrong (and you understand what that definition means!).
- You understand that everyone has an anger problem, that it can manifest itself in a host of forms and degrees, and that it is rarely righteous, although we often deceive ourselves to the contrary.
- You realize that God calls you, in dependence on his forgiving and empowering grace, to uproot anger from your heart.
- You have been given many specific strategies and steps for change on both the root and fruit levels.
- You know that you desperately need and marvelously have a Redeemer!

The natural question arises: What will motivate us to be a doer of God's Word? Why should we deal with our anger problems? Why should we, and our friends and family members, seek to uproot anger and replace it with godly fruit? In other words, what should move people to Christlike change?

In one sense, we must deal with sinful anger simply because God commands us to do so. We are responsible to put our sin to death (Rom. 8:13). Christ calls believers, in light of grace, to get rid of sinful anger and replace it with righteousness (Eph. 4:22–24, 31; Col. 3:8).

Furthermore, in Christ, God provides all we need to do so. His Spirit and his Word are sufficient to change us (Col. 2:9–10; 2 Tim. 3:16–17; 2 Peter 1:3). We must respond to God's grace by applying these provisions and actively obeying him. This requires Spirit-imparted commitment and effort (Phil. 2:12–13).

Yet Scripture provides more than broad principles. God supplies compelling motives to change our anger. Let's consider three pairs—positive and negative—of persuasive reasons why you should deal with your anger problems biblically. Each pair looks at the same matter from the perspective of warnings and promises, of curses and blessings.

Reason #1: Avoiding Injury to, and Promoting the Well-Being of, Your Physical and Spiritual Health

In one sense, of course, all sin is self-destructive. Long before the arrival of modern medicine, the Bible described the psychosomatic (or "spirituo-somatic") connection between sin and sickness, and between righteousness and health. Passages such as Psalms 32 and 38 and Proverbs 3 show this general link. Of particular importance is Proverbs 14:29–30, a text that addresses anger: "A patient man has great understanding, but a quick-tempered man displays folly. A heart at peace gives life to the body, but envy rots the bones." The Hebrew poetic structure suggests that the patience-versus-quick-tempered antithesis parallels the "life to the body" versus "rots the bones" antithesis.

In other words, both anger and envy damage the body, whereas the qualities of patience and peace bring health.

Centuries ago, the Puritan pastor-theologian Richard Baxter addressed this tie between anger and poor health: "Observe also what an enemy it [anger] is to the body itself. It inflameth the blood, and stirreth up diseases, and breedeth the strength of nature, and hath cast many into acute, and many into chronical sicknesses, which have proved their death. And how uncomfortable a kind of death is this!"[1]

Over the years, others have observed the same correlation between anger (particularly the concealed sort) and illness. Observers report an association between mismanaged anger and physiological consequences such as tension headaches, hypertension (high blood pressure), stomach ulcers, colitis, and even colds.

Kent learned this lesson by experience after separating from his wife. "I know my heart is not right toward God," he confided in our counseling session. "I am angry at Kathy. I'm very bitter. She has been awful to me for twelve years, and now she's doing the right thing and she's judging me." Kent was torn between what God wanted and his affection for another woman.

"How are things?" I began in our next session. "Things are getting worse. I'm going downhill." "How so?" I asked. Kent was honest: "I'm discouraged. I'm not sleeping, I'm losing weight, and I'm very tired physically and emotionally. My work is suffering. My supervisor is getting upset with me." "What do you want?" I pursued. "I want my walk with the Lord restored and these stomach pains to go away." Kent was a walking—or, better, limping—testimony of the truth of Proverbs 14. Sleep loss, weight loss, tiredness, and stomach pains attended his way.

Worse, spiritual consequences come when we fail to handle anger properly. We forfeit various spiritual blessings. For example, we relinquish a clear conscience before God and others and must contend with our guilt. It disrupts our peace with God: "So I strive always to keep my conscience clear before God and man" (Acts 24:16). No blessing is more precious to the believer than a clear conscience (cf. 1 Cor. 4:1–5; 2 Cor. 1:12; 1 Tim. 1:18–20).

In addition, anger hinders our prayer life and our communion with God:

- If I had cherished sin in my heart, the Lord would not have listened. . . . (Ps. 66:18).
- I want men everywhere to lift up holy hands in prayer, without anger or disputing. (1 Tim. 2:8)
- Husbands, in the same way be considerate as you live with your wives, and treat them with respect as the weaker partner and as heirs with you of the gracious gift of life, so that nothing will hinder your prayers. (1 Peter 3:7)

Do you want God's ear inclined toward you when you pray? Then repent of your anger.

Furthermore, sinful anger exposes us to divine judgment: "You have heard that it was said to the people long ago, 'Do not murder, and anyone who murders will be subject to judgment.' But I tell you that anyone who is angry with his brother will be subject to judgment. Again, anyone who says to his brother, 'Raca,' is answerable to the Sanhedrin. But anyone who says, 'You fool!' will be in danger of the fire of hell" (Matt. 5:21–22; cf. 1 John 3:15).

While there is no condemnation for those who are in Christ (Rom. 8:1), unrepentant anger patterns may rightly call into question the credibility of the so-called believer's profession of faith. On the other hand, growth in Christlikeness, including progress in changing sinful anger, adds confidence to our assurance of salvation (1 John 2:3–6).

Finally, as it did with Cain, unrestrained anger makes us prey to the enslaving power of sin that wants greater mastery over us: "Then the LORD said to Cain, 'Why are you angry? Why is your face downcast? If you do what is right, will you not be accepted? But if you do not do what is right, sin is crouching at your door; it desires to have you, but you must master it' " (Gen. 4:6–7).

> **Physical and Spiritual Health Consequences**
> * Physical health problems (psychosomatic effects)
> * Spiritual health problems
> * Unclear conscience
> * Clouded prayers/ communion with God
> * Divine judgment
> * Enslaving power of sinful anger

Along these lines, Frederick Buechner pointedly observes: "Of the seven deadly sins, anger is probably the most fun. To lick your wounds, smack your lips over grievances long past, roll over your tongue the prospect of bitter confrontation still to come, to savor to the last toothsome morsel both the pain you are given and the pain you are giving back—is a feast fit for a king. The chief drawback is that what you are wolfing down is yourself. The skeleton at the feast is you."[2]

An additional avenue of biblical evidence comes from the book of Proverbs. The writer promises a multitude of blessings or curses to individuals who walk wisely or foolishly. God gives straightforward, blunt commands to his creatures. Read Proverbs, starting in chapter 1, and the refrain will overwhelm you: it is *good* for you to heed God's voice; it is *bad* for you to ignore it. Dealing with anger God's way will enhance your physical and spiritual health.

Reason #2: Avoiding Damage to, and Promoting Growth in, Your Interpersonal Relationships

Your anger keeps you from loving your neighbor as yourself. It injures and alienates people. It hinders the establishment and growth of godly friendships. On the other hand, dealing with anger, resolving conflicts, and reconciling hurts strengthen and sweeten all your relationships.

Several passages demonstrate this connection. Paul calls us to deal with our anger in Ephesians 4:26–27: " 'In your anger do not sin': Do not let the sun go down while you are still angry, and do not give the devil a foothold." He continues in verse 31, "Get rid of all bitterness, rage and anger, brawling and slander, along with every form of malice." Likewise, Colossians 3:8 exhorts us, "But now you must rid yourselves of all such things as these: anger, rage, malice, slander, and filthy language from your lips."

What does this have to do with interpersonal relationships? Both of these sets of injunctions against anger emerge in the broader contexts of "one another" relationships (Eph. 4:1–6; 4:25–5:2; Col. 3:5–17).

In other words, failure to get rid of anger prevents the proper unity, functioning, and growth of Christ's body. It divides and cuts his church. At the same time, these same passages hold out the attractiveness of people communing together in genuine love, forgiveness, and mutual concern.

The apostle James's exhortations to repent, explored in chapter 3 above, also involve relationships within the church. The bitter envy, selfish ambition, and entrenched desires that he addresses in James 3:13–4:12 breed disorder, conflict, and slander within interpersonal relationships. Instead, he bids us to see the beauty of a better way of associating with one another: "But the wisdom that comes from heaven is first of all pure; then peace-loving, considerate, submissive, full of mercy and good fruit, impartial and sincere. Peacemakers who sow in peace raise a harvest of righteousness" (James 3:17–18).

Perhaps no single sentence strikes this point more forcefully than Luke 15:28: "The older brother became angry and refused to go in." In his anger, he distanced himself from people. While his brother had previously squandered his wealth, this man now squandered his opportunity to love his repentant brother and his happy father. Sadly, he refused to move toward them in meaningful relationship. He forfeited the joy of celebrating this reunion with his family and friends. Worse, he dishonored his dad.

> Pursuing relational peace requires uprooting personal anger!

Gus and Gail illustrate a common relational scenario. They went to their pastor for marriage counseling to "restore peace" and "improve communication." For three years, Gus's chronic outbursts, red-faced reactions, and shouting had shattered all intimacy between them. Every serious conversation degenerated into conflict. Even seemingly safe topics mushroomed into arguments. They had pursued independent lifestyles. Sexual union had ceased. Gail was sleeping in the guest room. Only the presence of children prevented divorce.

By God's grace, Gus began to see his sinfulness. He had failed to be a Christlike learner, lover, and leader of his wife. The truths in chapter 3 about his angry heart-idols gripped him. He became painfully aware of how his words had pierced Gail and how his reckless venting had pushed her away. He had acted like a "worthless bum," and he knew it. Now, with the Spirit's help, he began to make marked progress along the path of repentance, faith, and obedience. Gus learned to move toward Gail, relationally, with gentleness, wisdom, and sensitivity.

Gail, however, faced a difficult crossroads. On the one hand, she genuinely appreciated Gus's growth. "Finally," she remarked, "I'm getting the kind of husband I have always wanted, the kind of man I knew Gus could be." Yet Gail soon discovered a part of her heart previously hidden to her. She saw her bitterness and judgmentalism. As long as Gus had mistreated her, she justified her coldness in the name of self-protection. Self-righteously, she savored her victimhood.

Now, however, those many years of concealed anger stared back at her with icy eyes. Could she—would she—forgive her

159

repentant husband? Would she respond to Gus by moving toward him? Would she risk opening her life to him again? Or would she remain distant? Would she place him on probation? Would she raise some unreachable penitential hoops through which Gus would not be able to jump?

I wish I could report a positive conclusion to Gail's story. Sadly, unlike Jill in our previous case study, her bitterness never broke. She withdrew from counseling.

Yet all this created a new test for Gus. It was one thing to repent while Gail remained committed; it was another thing to love her when she rejected him. Would he continue to love her with his budding Christlike love, even if she did not reciprocate? Or would he in anger turn away from her and become bitter like her? Thankfully, Gus continued on the path of repentance, to please Christ more than to win back Gail. But the road has been hard.

Anger, in both its revealed and concealed forms, damages relationships. It severs marriages and alienates families. It keeps us from reconciling relationships and pursuing peace. Sinful anger excuses our planks and highlights others' specks (Matt. 7:3–5).

The wisdom writer recognized the infectious nature of anger in Proverbs 22:24–25: "Do not make friends with a hot-tempered man, do not associate with one easily angered, for you may learn his ways and get yourself ensnared."

Our anger not only hurts others, but also provokes their anger. It models and tempts those around us to clam or to vent. It is no wonder that the Proverbs writers issue young people so many warnings about the negative effects of ungodly people. And it is no wonder that the apostle Paul in Ephesians 6:4 warns dads that their own sinfulness, including anger (4:26–27, 31), can provoke their children to anger. Anger elicits anger; venters incite venters.

At the same time, dealing with your anger increases the likelihood of God's using you to improve relationships with others.

- When a man's ways are pleasing to the LORD, he makes even his enemies live at peace with him. (Prov. 16:7)
- You hypocrite, first take the plank out of your own eye, and then you will see clearly to remove the speck from your brother's eye. (Matt. 7:5)
- If it is possible, as far as it depends on you, live at peace with everyone. (Rom. 12:18)

Sinful anger, therefore, not only hurts me (reason #1). It also hurts others (reason #2). It prevents edification and ruins relationships. Anger divides families, separates friends, and alienates church members. We must deal with it to love others and promote godly relationships. By doing so, we bring grace, healing, and hope to those around us.

Reason #3: Avoiding God's Displeasure and Bringing Him Honor and Delight

The worst result of anger, for the Christian, is that it dishonors, displeases, and offends your Lord. As we have seen, God's Word certainly urges you to get rid of sinful anger because it injures both your health and your relationships. Secular therapists appeal to their clients by advancing similar lines of arguments.

Yet these are not the Bible's highest motives. The preeminent rationale for biblical change—for replacing anger with godly fruit—concerns our relationship to God our Savior. The most pressing biblical questions are not "What does unresolved anger do to me? How does it affect my relationships?" but "What will it do to my Lord? How does it grieve him? What does he think about me and my anger problem?"

161

As the moral equivalent of murder (Matt. 5:21–22), anger violates Christ's commands. "Anyone who hates his brother is a murderer, and you know that no murderer has eternal life in him" (1 John 3:15). Anger is disobedience to our Savior and incites his judgment. On the flip side, repenting of sinful anger, and loving and praying for our enemies, imitates our Father in heaven (Matt. 5:43–48) and brings him praise from others (5:13–16).

In Ephesians 4:26–27, Paul warns us to deal rightly with our anger lest we "give the devil a foothold." Unresolved anger affords Satan a port of entry into the church's life. It is a way in which believers, sadly, side with God's archenemy. We further the evil one's destructive agenda to destroy God's people.

In addition, the apostle calls us to "get rid of all bitterness, rage and anger, brawling and slander, along with every form of malice" (v. 31). Interestingly, Paul contextually precedes this injunction with verse 30, which urges us, "And do not grieve the Holy Spirit of God, with whom you were sealed for the day of redemption." The worst consequence of anger is neither colitis nor divorce but the grieving of God himself! Yet learning to display truthfulness, kindness, forgiveness, and love makes us like the Father and the Son (Eph. 4:20–5:2).

The parallel passage in Colossians 3:5–11 conveys the same truths. Verse 8 commands believers to "rid yourselves of all such things as these: anger, rage, malice, slander, and filthy language from your lips." Why? Paul roots the motivation in our relationship to God. These are the kinds of behaviors that invite God's wrath against the ungodly (v. 6). They are incompatible with the new life that God has given us, contrary to his image, and opposed to his goal of re-creating us into that image (vv. 7, 10–11). To cling to our anger is to work at cross-purposes with God's agenda of making us like him. To repent of our anger is to participate in his glorious goal.

In 1 Timothy 2:8, the same apostle declares, "I want men everywhere to lift up holy hands in prayer, without anger or disputing." The context deals with the activity of public worship and the ordering of local congregational life. In such a setting, anger hinders the worship of God. To paraphrase Isaiah 29:13, these men honor God with their lips and holy hands, but their angry hearts are far from him!

Perhaps the passage that shows our third point most clearly is James 1:19–20: "My dear brothers, take note of this: Everyone should be quick to listen, slow to speak and slow to become angry, for man's anger does not bring about the righteous life that God desires."

The apostle calls us to be "quick to listen, slow to speak and slow to become angry." Why? Why must we get rid of our sinful anger? Not because it will damage our health or ruin our relationships (although it might do both), but because it dishonors, displeases, and offends God! As James writes, "man's anger does not bring about the righteous life that God desires" (v. 20).

Several observations are useful. First, James makes a general statement that human anger is sinful. He does not qualify is as "man's *sinful* anger." James assumes that human anger is sinful. (Righteous anger is an exception to that rule and is not in view here.)

Second, and centrally, our anger falls short of what God desires us to be. It displeases the Lord. It is contrary to his agenda of maturing in Christ. Anger is unlike God. It is unlike his Son, who has purchased us and now owns us. The highest cause for a Christian to change his anger is to please God and bring him praise (2 Cor. 5:9).

Do you want to bring delight to God—to satisfy his desires? Then root out your anger and replace it with Christlikeness.

Third, as most commentators observe, the context suggests a gathering for worship and/or public teaching of God's Word.

163

If so, then we must pay special attention to ways in which our sinful anger—quick tempers, grudges, and the like—becomes an obstacle to such worship and teaching. We must be sensitive to occasions for anger before, during, and after the congregational gathering, including the tensions we may have toward others within the body of Christ.

For example, our closet and congregational pre-worship prayer foci should regularly include repentance over anger. We must pray for ourselves and our families, and for our church families, as we are getting dressed and preparing to leave our houses to attend Lord's Day congregational gatherings. Tensions can easily erupt at home or on the way to worship.

A final text from James, discussed in chapter 3, merits consideration. In James 4:11–12, the apostle warns against judgmentalism and slander, a root-and-fruit combination within the anger constellation. Why is such behavior wrong? Not because it hurts you, although it will. And not even because it offends others, although it does. It's wrong because it usurps *God's* role as Lawgiver and Judge. It grabs at his throne. Ultimately, anger is not about us or about others; it's about God.

Anger, as God-playing, is of the worst moral evil. To repent of anger is to acknowledge God's rightful and sole place as King over your entire world.

While secular writers miss this theological dimension, sadly, most Christian "integrationist" authors do also. They fail to see anger as primarily sin against God. They instead minimize, euphemize, rationalize, or neutralize anger.

For example, one popular book on anger, written by a well-known Christian psychologist and now in its third edition, essentially ignores God. The writer does not even refer to the book of James or related passages. God's presence is noticeably absent. The reason anger is bad is that it damages my health and my relationships, but not that it offends my God. The motive to change, in turn, becomes self-centered: to please myself or others, not my Creator and Redeemer. There is no call to have dealings with God or to mourn over and repent of grieving him.

STUART: CHANGING WITHOUT GOD?

Stuart's case exemplifies this error. Five years ago, he suffered a major job setback. From his perspective, a team of employers who were prominent Christian leaders had mistreated him. They yanked his career plans out from under him; they dashed his hopes. The mistreatment eventually resulted in his reluctant resignation. From then on, Stuart struggled with the mistreatment itself. Furthermore, the mistreatment included several charges against him that had damaged his reputation, questioned his credibility, and hindered his career pursuits.

Consumed with hurt, Stuart came to me as a friend and a pastor. His intake form showed a desire for help with "conflict resolution," "frustration," "needed closure," and "forgiveness." It didn't note the depth of anger we were soon to unpack.

Although Stuart had left the company, he continued to sow and reap a harvest of lingering problems: bitterness against the employers for their wrongful treatment; thoughts of covert and overt acts of revenge; gnawing yet undetected guilt over his own sinful responses; ongoing frustration over an unfavorable public reputation; and general confusion about what to do next.

How did counseling begin? Extensive data-gathering reconstructed a detailed chronology of the conflict events. Stuart described and documented a sad scene. I acknowledged the hurt he had experienced and the severe ways in which he had been sinned against. I laid a biblical foundation of hope as we discussed God's sovereignty, justice, goodness, and forgiveness. Stuart's intellectual understanding was theologically sound; he was struggling to apply it.

Having secured Stuart's commitment to seek to please God, I laid out a biblical model for conflict resolution. The model would lead to a wise and sincere effort to reconcile with these employers. We mapped out a practical game plan for our counseling sessions and agreed to proceed accordingly.

We began with a Matthew 7:3–5 "plank list" of Stuart's wrong behavior before, during, and after the conflict. This included several forms of concealed and revealed anger. We exposed several lies and lusts that had ruled, and were continuing to rule, his heart.

The critical test came when I asked Stuart to write a prayer of repentance to God over his sinful fruit and roots. What emerged was a mixture of confession and blame-shifting: "Lord Jesus, . . . I realize that I did not respond entirely to what is taught in Scripture when one faces *people who are unloving, selfish, and divisive. . . .* Lord, forgive me *if* I was insubordinate. . . . Please forgive me *if* I have done anything to hurt the cause of Christ" (emphasis mine).

A second and a third attempt, even after continued scriptural correction and instruction, yielded similar results. There was no clear confession of sin but ongoing accusation against his enemies. Stuart remained ruled by bitterness against them and blindness about his own evil. What his enemies had done to him troubled him far more than what he had done to God and to them (Matt 18:21–35). He eventually admitted, "I have a hard time admitting my sin."

What went wrong? Stuart had a motive problem. In each session, I probed, instructed, and confronted him concerning self-centered motives. Stuart wanted a biblical counselor who would vindicate his "righteous" cause. He wanted reconciliation not because he had offended God and others but because this conflict was blocking his vocational advancement. He wanted these employers exposed. Stuart also wanted to feel better. He was suffering the burden and pressure of an unresolved past. It was eating away at him and affecting his marriage and current work and ministry performance.

What Stuart missed was the fact that his anger—in both its fruit and root—was first and foremost sin against God (Ps. 51:3–4). He failed to grasp the exceeding sinfulness of his anger in God's eyes, before God's face (*coram Deo*). His sin violated both God's law and God's grace. Thankfully, Stuart eventually came to see these realities, to own his sin against the living God and the need to uproot his anger. So must you and I.

SUMMARY

Sinful anger injures your physical and spiritual health. It damages your interpersonal relationships. Yet as Stuart eventually learned, the greatest reason to change your anger is that it displeases, dishonors, and offends the Savior who died and rose for you. No higher motive exists for you and me, and our friends and family members, to change and grow. By doing so, we bring God great honor and delight. We please God by obeying him and becoming like his Son. May God be pleased to work his sanctifying grace in us!

"May the God of peace, who through the blood of the eternal covenant brought back from the dead our Lord Jesus, that great Shepherd of the sheep, equip you with everything good for doing his will, and may he work in us what is pleasing to him, through Jesus Christ, to whom be glory for ever and ever. Amen" (Heb. 13:20–21).

For Further Reflection and Life Application

1. Test this chapter's thesis by individually polling a group of Christians. Ask them what's the biggest reason why people need to deal with their anger problems. See how many, if any, responses point to pleasing and not griev-

ing God. Then recommit yourself to making God the focal point of both your own fight against anger and your ministry toward others.

2. Can you sympathize with Stuart above? There are many men and women like him. Have you been mistreated or severely mistreated, and found it difficult to restrain your anger? You are not alone. Fix your eyes on him who endured both the unrighteous wrath of man and the righteous wrath of God to save your soul and secure your eternal union with him.

3. Think globally. If pursuing relational peace requires uprooting personal anger, how do we think of various efforts—diplomatic or military—to end civil wars in other nations? What motivates international leaders to pursue peace, and how would we compare and contrast that peace with the peace that God holds out in the gospel and his church?

Appendix A
SAMPLE GROWTH AND
APPLICATION ASSIGNMENTS

The following pages contain six sample homework assignment forms that I often use in counseling angry people. Suggestions about how to use them appear in chapter 9. These may be reproduced, in the form presented, for personal ministry use.

1. Journaling a Problem Incident
2. Inventory of Personal Felt Needs and Rights
3. James 4 and the Cause of Conflicts
4. Controlling Your Angry Behavior
5. Pictures of God's Forgiveness of His People
6. Battling Bitterness with the Gospel

JOURNALING A PROBLEM INCIDENT

Select a recent incident in which you displayed or felt anger, conflict, depression, anxiety, or similar negative attitudes or actions. Then summarize the situation and your response to it:

1. **Your Situation.** Who, what, where, when? Summarize what happened:

2. **Your Behavior.** What did you say, do, and feel in response to what happened? Summarize your words, actions, and emotions, especially the negative ones:

3. **Your Thoughts and Desires.** What were you thinking or wanting in the midst of this situation? Summarize your attitudes, thoughts, desires, motives, etc., that might have driven the wrong behavior. Note any "good desire, bad master" dynamics.

4. **God's Answers.** On the back of this sheet, describe how you think God would want you to deal with this situation now or the next time it occurs. What changes in your behavior and in your thoughts, desires, and motives seem needed? What steps should you take?

INVENTORY OF PERSONAL FELT NEEDS AND RIGHTS

Personal or relational problems often arise when we feel that our personal needs or rights are unmet or denied. Examining these feelings gives insight into our problems and God's solutions.[1]

Step #1: Identify Your Felt Needs or Rights. Check each item that you view as a personal need or right (or intense desire). You may add brief explanatory notes.

1. Be free of intense problems and pressures
2. Privacy
3. Hold and express personal opinions
4. Have money/possessions and use them as you choose
5. Plan my daily schedule
6. Be respected, appreciated, considered important
7. Friends, close relationships
8. Be loved and accepted
9. Be understood, listened to
10. Be supported and cared for
11. Make my own decisions
12. Plan my future
13. Good health, adequate medical care
14. Date or marry
15. Loving, caring, committed spouse
16. Sexual fulfillment
17. Children
18. Raise children the way you choose
19. Children who obey, respect, appreciate you
20. Children who work hard and succeed in school/job/marriage
21. Be successful in job, family, or church
22. Satisfying employment, enjoying your job

23. Affirmation from your employer
24. Day off from work
25. Coworkers respect, appreciate you
26. Personal hopes and aspirations fulfilled
27. Be treated fairly
28. Have fun in life
29. Be physically protected, secure
30. Other:

Step #2: Identify Your Unmet Needs or Denied Rights. Circle the numbers of items above that are currently unmet/denied.

Step #3: Prioritize Your Most Urgent Unmet Needs/Denied Rights. Describe your two most pressing unmet needs or denied rights:

1. Right/need:

   Unmet/denied by whom?

   How? In what way?

   How do you tend to respond or act toward this person?

2. Right/need:

   Unmet/denied by whom?

   How? In what way?

   How do you tend to respond or act toward this person?

JAMES 4 AND THE CAUSE OF CONFLICTS

Understanding God's Truth

1. Carefully read James 3:13–4:12 twice.
2. What major problems do 3:16, 4:1a, and 4:2 address?
3. What are the causes or sources of conflicts, quarrels, and fights in 4:1–3?
4. What makes these desires sinful in 4:1–3? For example, is it because you want *bad things* or because you want good things *too much* (inordinate desires)? 4:2 gives a clue.
5. List additional observations about sinful desires in James 1:13–16; 3:13–18; 4:4–12.
6. What does 4:4–12 counsel you to do concerning your sinful desires?

Applying God's Truth

1. Briefly describe a current or recent conflict situation.
2. Describe your desires in this situation. What did you/do you want to have happen or not to have happen?
3. How did/do these desires lead you to wrong words, actions, or feelings?
4. Analyze these desires by placing them in one or more of the following categories:
   (a) Desires for wrong objects, bad things.
   (b) Desires for good objects, but for selfish reasons, or desires that are too strong—inordinate, ruling, controlling, "must have" desires (a "good desire, bad master" dynamic). (Note: Desires rule you if they consume your thoughts, if you sin to get them, or if you sin when you don't get them.)
5. What do you think God wants you to do about your desires that produce conflict? What practical steps should you take to deal with them?

CONTROLLING YOUR ANGRY BEHAVIOR:
A BIBLE STUDY ASSIGNMENT FROM PROVERBS

God's Word presents a twofold strategy for overcoming sinful anger: recognize and root out its source on the heart level, and control its expression on the behavioral level (words and actions). This assignment focuses on this second aspect—learning to control the expression of your anger. Carefully read each verse from Proverbs, meditate on it, and answer the following questions.

Prov. 29:11: "A fool gives full vent to his anger, but a wise man keeps himself under control."

1. How does a fool handle his anger?

2. How does a wise man handle it?

3. What are some ways in which you might control and not vent your anger?

4. Memorize this verse. Whenever you're tempted to vent your anger, repeat it to yourself five times.

Prov. 14:16-17: "A wise man fears the LORD and shuns evil, but a fool is hotheaded and reckless. A quick-tempered man does foolish things, and a crafty man is hated."

1. How is a fool described? What does he do?

2. How is a wise man described?

Prov. 14:29–30: "A patient man has great understanding, but a quick-tempered man displays folly. A heart at peace gives life to the body, but envy rots the bones."

1. How is an angry man described?

2. What is the opposite of a fool? How is he described?

3. Could anger produce physical problems?

Prov. 15:1: "A gentle answer turns away wrath, but a harsh word stirs up anger."

1. How should we respond to anger?

2. What does this produce?

3. Give an example:

4. What does a harsh response produce?

Prov. 15:18: "A hot-tempered man stirs up dissension, but a patient man calms a quarrel."

1. How does anger contribute to conflicts?

2. How does a patient man calm conflicts?

3. How can you develop patience?

Prov. 16:32: "Better a patient man than a warrior, a man who controls his temper than one who takes a city."

Describe (and meditate on) the image of strength that this verse gives:

Prov. 19:11: "A man's wisdom gives him patience; it is to his glory to overlook an offense."

What temper-controlling activity is mentioned here?

Prov. 19:19: "A hot-tempered man must pay the penalty; if you rescue him, you will have to do it again."

1. What penalty must the angry man pay?

2. Why?

Prov. 22:24-25: "Do not make friends with a hot-tempered man, do not associate with one easily angered, or you may learn his ways and get yourself ensnared."

1. What danger is there in associating with an angry person?

2. What does this imply about our own anger?

Prov. 29:9: "If a wise man goes to court with a fool, the fool rages and scoffs, and there is no peace."

What does a fool do amid conflict?

Prov. 29:20: "Do you see a man who speaks in haste? There is more hope for a fool than for him."

What aspect of uncontrolled anger is mentioned?

Prov. 29:22: "An angry man stirs up dissension, and a hot-tempered one commits many sins."

What results from anger?

PICTURES OF GOD'S FORGIVENESS OF HIS PEOPLE

Read each passage carefully and prayerfully. For each, list any word pictures or images of God's forgiveness, along with personal applications or questions you have. Write a brief applicational response (What is God saying to me?).

Psalm 103:8–14

Psalm 130:3–4

Isaiah 1:18

Isaiah 38:17

Isaiah 43:25

Isaiah 44:21–22

Jeremiah 31:31–34

Jeremiah 50:20

Micah 7:18–20

1. Examine each passage below and briefly write down what it teaches about forgiving your offender in your heart before God, i.e., having a forgiving attitude in which you repent of your bitterness, release him from your judgment, and refuse to hold his sin against him.

Genesis 50:19–20

Micah 6:6–8

Matthew 5:3–10

Matthew 6:9–15

Matthew 18:21–35

Mark 11:20–25

Luke 6:32–36

Luke 23:32–34

Acts 7:54–60

Romans 12:17–21

Ephesians 4:30–5:2

Colossians 3:12–13

James 2:12–13

James 4:11–12

2. Based on these passages, list reasons why God wants you to forgive your offender attitudinally, in your heart. (Note: one way to organize these same passages has been provided for you on page 105)

3. Write out, memorize, and recite Ephesians 4:32 when thoughts of your offender enter your mind.

Appendix B
RECONSIDERING TWO "ANGER" TEXTS: EPHESIANS 4:26 AND HEBREWS 12:15

Counseling ourselves or others biblically requires not only a commitment to apply God's Word to ourselves and others but also a prior commitment to understand God's Word properly. The following two verses are sometimes cited by popular Bible teachers and Christian counselors, in ways that are arguably questionable or inaccurate.

EPHESIANS 4:26: COMMAND OR CONCESSION?

New Testament exegetes debate the meaning of the first half of Ephesians 4:26 (4:26a), "Be angry, and yet do not sin" (NASB). Here is the Greek text and five of the most popular English translations:

- *Orgizesthe kai mē hamartanete: ho hēlios mē epiduetō epi parorgismō humōn,*
- NIV: "In your anger do not sin": Do not let the sun go down while you are still angry.
- NASB (rev. 1995): Be angry, and yet do not sin; do not let the sun go down on your anger. . . .
- KJV: Be ye angry, and sin not: let not the sun go down upon your wrath. . . .

181

- NKJV: "Be angry, and do not sin": do not let the sun go down on your wrath. . . .
- ESV: Be angry and do not sin; do not let the sun go down on your anger. . . .

The crux of the debate centers on translating the verb *orgizesthe*, the imperatival form of *orgizomai*, "to be angry." Does it carry volative (command) or concessive force?

Two major views are commonly held.[1] English versions such as the NASB, ESV, NKJV, and KJV above translate it as a command. This is the view of several commentators.[2] English versions such as the NIV, however, translate it as a concession: " 'In your anger do not sin': Do not let the sun go down while you are still angry." This is the position of the majority of the standard New Testament Greek reference books, along with many commentators and communicators.[3] Proponents cite similar concessive imperatives in Ecclesiastes 11:9, Matthew 23:32, John 2:19, 7:52, and 2 Corinthians 12:16.

This second view seems preferable for several reasons. First, it better fits the contextual flow of the passage, especially in light of verse 31's blanket condemnation of all anger: "Get rid of all bitterness, rage and anger, brawling and slander, along with every form of malice." To call for righteous anger in the context of 4:17–32 seems out of place. Second, while righteous anger is certainly encouraged by biblical example (as in chapter 2 of our book), in no other place does the Bible command believers to be angry. If this is a command for righteous anger, it is a singular example in the Bible. Third, the weight and virtual unanimity of New Testament Greek scholarship is persuasive. As one writer summarizes it, "It is quite wrong to take it as a command or even a permission to be angry."[4]

What implications flow from adopting this concessive translation? Does this verse permit, or even encourage, anger? Does

182

it allow for righteous anger? Andrew Lincoln gives wise answers that every pastor and biblical counselor should heed:

> It is usually agreed that the first imperative in this formulation should be construed as having concessive force. . . . It is important, however, to be clear about the force of this construction. It is *not granting permission* to be angry. Although v26b recognizes that anger will occur, v27 indicates how dangerous it is and v31 repudiates all anger (cf. also 6:4). The focus of v26a, then, is on not sinning by indulging in anger. Its paradoxical formulation was *not meant to encourage speculation about what types of anger might be permissible.* Whatever the merits of the traditional notion of righteous anger at injustice or the modern notion of the healthiness of expressing rather than suppressing anger, they should *not be thought to have support in the concessive aspect of this prohibition.* Its force may be conveyed by a paraphrase, "Anger is to be avoided at all costs, but if, for whatever reason, you do get angry, then refuse to indulge such anger so that you do not sin." In this way, the exhortation is very much in line with the view of anger elsewhere in the NT.[5]

Lincoln then cites Matthew 5:22; Galatians 5:20; Colossians 3:8; 1 Timothy 2:8; Titus 1:7; and James 1:19–20 as constituting a New Testament view of anger.

H. C. Hahn, in *The New International Dictionary of New Testament Theology,* captures this same sense in this paraphrase: "But where a man has become angry *(whether for good or bad reasons),* he is not to let the sun set on his anger."[6] In other words, the author's intent in verse 26a is not to command anger, not to rule on the rightness or wrongness of the given anger, and not to declare anger to be some neutral, amoral emotion ("neither good nor bad; it just is"). His purpose is to direct Christians how to deal with their anger.

While the above argument may not persuade all Bible teachers and Christian counselors to abandon their anger-is-commanded interpretation of Ephesians 4:26, it is my hope that it will at least drive us all to restudy this passage, to hold our view less tenaciously, and to build our theology of righteous anger on a more solid basis than this debatable text. May God drive each of us to constant reexamination of his Word and to more skillful ministry of that Word to ourselves and others.

HEBREWS 12:15 AND THE ROOT OF BITTERNESS

To diagnose the problem of bitterness and to warn people against unresolved anger, a number of popular Bible teachers and popular Christian counselors adopt a questionable interpretation of Hebrews 12:15. I've reproduced the Greek text below along with five popular English translations, emphasizing the key phrase each time.

- *Episkopountes mē tis husterōn apo tēs chariots tō Theou, mē tis rhiza pikrias anō phuousa enochlē kai dia tautēs mianthōsin hoi polloi,*
- NIV: See to it that no one misses the grace of God and that no *bitter root* grows up to cause trouble and defile many.
- NASB (rev. 1995): See to it that no one comes short of the grace of God; that no *root of bitterness* springing up causes trouble, and by it many be defiled. . . .
- KJV: Looking diligently lest any man fail of the grace of God; lest any *root of bitterness* springing up trouble you, and thereby many be defiled. . . .
- NKJV: looking carefully lest anyone fall short of the grace of God; lest any *root of bitterness* springing up cause trouble, and by this many become defiled. . . .

- ESV: See to it that no one fails to obtain the grace of God; that no *"root of bitterness"* springs up and causes trouble, and by it many become defiled. . . .

Based on the phrase "root of bitterness," a number of teachers and counselors assert that unreconciled anger can settle down into someone's heart and produce "bitterness." That bitterness then takes "root" inside, and in turn produces all sorts of personal and relational problems. Change comes not by making mere behavioral adjustments but by dealing with that bitterness on the root level, in the person's heart.

Is this what Hebrews 12:15 teaches? No.

The purpose of the epistle to the Hebrews, according to 13:22, is to exhort and encourage God's people to cling to Jesus Christ and his new-covenant way of salvation, and to not revert to their former old-covenant ways. The unnamed apostle accomplishes this by making numerous arguments that present the superiority of Jesus and his new way over the Levitical system of the law of Moses. He regularly supports his arguments with citations and allusions to Old Testament texts and to events in Israel's history. He frequently presses his application with explicit commands to persevere in faith, love, and obedience to Christ, coupled with severe warnings about the consequences of apostasy.

In Hebrews 12:14–17, the writer resumes his exhortation. In verse 14, he calls his Christian community to pursue peace and holiness. Then in verse 15, he urges church members to make sure of two things: first, that none of them "misses" (NIV; or "fails of," KJV; "fall[s] short of," NKJV; "comes short of," NASB; "fails to obtain," ESV) God's grace now given them in the new covenant; and second, that no "root of bitterness" (or "bitter root," NIV) grows up among them to cause trouble and defilement.

185

What is this "root of bitterness" (*rhiza pikrias*)? The apostle alludes to Deuteronomy 29:18 (28:17 in the Hebrew Masoretic text and the Greek Septuagint), where Moses warns the nation of Israel to make sure that no one—man or woman—among them turns away from the Lord to serve other gods (as in vv. 16–18).[7] "Make sure there is no man or woman, clan or tribe among you today whose heart turns away from the LORD our God to go and worship the gods of those nations; make sure there is no root among you that produces such bitter poison" (Deut. 29:18). Such a person would be like a root or shoot growing up among the congregation and bearing "bitter poison" (NIV; "poisonous and bitter fruit," ESV; "poisonous fruit and wormwood," NASB) that will lead others astray. As one commentator observes, "The image of a bitter root that can spread to infect many is from Deuteronomy 29:18. . . . The text in Deuteronomy is quite appropriate, for it refers to apostasy, as the writer of Hebrews does."[8]

This Deuteronomy allusion supports what appears to be a natural understanding of Hebrews 12:15, namely, that the apostle's new-covenant-community readers must take responsibility that no one among them miss God's grace and turn away from the Lord Jesus. In other words, verse 15 is a warning against apostasy and a call to members of the congregation to take spiritual oversight of one another. This, of course, fits the immediate context of Hebrews 12:14–17 and larger contexts of Hebrews 12 and the entire epistle. In verses 16–17, the apostle cites the example of Esau's rejection of God's grace. The writer of Hebrews is fond of citing Old Testament passages (such as Deut. 29:18) and characters (such as Esau) to warn against apostasy.

Hebrews 12:15 is a warning against apostasy that defiles the community. David Peterson agrees: "Christians are to be watchful about the spiritual welfare of others in the church, taking care that *no one misses the grace of God* (lit. 'falls short of God's grace'). God's grace is always available 'to help us in our time of need' (4:16). Those who fail to depend on it and respond to it will not enter his heavenly kingdom (cf. 3:12–14). Indeed, they may become a *bitter root* that causes trouble for the whole congregation and defiles many. Such imagery recalls Deut. 29:18, where Moses warns about the bitterness that can be spread throughout the community of God's people by one rebellious member."[9] Other commentators on Hebrews concur.[10]

Given this understanding of the text in its context, we can see several errors in the bitterness-in-your-heart understanding of Hebrews 12:15. In general, it misses the apostle's against-apostasy argument in the Hebrews 12 context and the purpose of the allusion to Deuteronomy 29:18.

Specifically, while this interpretation rightly understands the metaphorical use of the word "root" in Hebrews 12:15, it misses that meaning of "bitterness." Here, as in Deuteronomy 29:18, it has nothing to do with anger. It, too, is part of the metaphor and refers to the foul-tasting, noxious nature of the root (cf. James 3:11–12; Rev. 8:11). While the NIV's "bitter root" is less likely to be misread, an ideal English translation that would not risk the dual meaning of "bitterness" in our day might simply be "foul-tasting" or the like.

Furthermore, this popular interpretation unduly individualizes the passage. It sees the bitter root to lie in an individual's heart, with the root springing up from within the person's soul to then affect his whole life. But the flow of the argument in both Hebrews 12 and Deuteronomy 29 is corporate. The church body is to watch out that no person among them goes apostate. Such a person himself is viewed as the bitter root, not his heart. And the damage that the bitter root would cause is not individual struggles but tempting the congregation to idolatry.

187

Does this mean that it's wrong to speak of anger as a root? No. It means that we must not read that notion into Hebrews 12:15, thereby missing its true meaning. This book's title, *Uprooting Anger*, emerges from a biblical theology of the heart as causative of human behavior, and passages such as Matthew 12:33–37, Jeremiah 17:5–10, and Luke 6:43–45 use fruit and tree/root metaphors to describe that connection.

NOTES

Chapter 1: What Is Anger?

1. Calling anger an "emotion" may misleadingly focus on affect and feelings in distinction from cognitive and volitional functions. As English dictionaries assert and daily speech affirms, we routinely speak of "emotion" as affect and feeling: "She reacted with much emotion"; "Don't let your emotions get the best of you"; "He needs to be more rational and less emotional about all this." Given this popular sense, the term "emotion" misses anger's whole-personed dynamic, especially the judgmental component that, as we shall see, lies at the core of anger. Some writers who concur with the holistic nature of anger, however, do use the term "emotion" as a summary label for anger (and depression, etc.) but also in the more narrow sense of affect and feelings. See the helpful articles by Sam R. Williams, "Toward a Theology of Emotion," *Southern Baptist Journal of Theology* 7:4 (Winter 2003), and David A. Powlison, "What Do You Feel?," *Journal of Biblical Counseling* 10:4 (1992).

2. Carol Tavris, *Anger: The Misunderstood Emotion* (New York: Simon and Schuster, 1982), 23. Emphasis mine.

3. David A. Powlison, "Anger Part 1: Understanding Anger," *Journal of Biblical Counseling*, 14:1 (1995): 48.

4. Elsie Johnson, in *Theological Dictionary of the Old Testament*, vol. 1, 2d ed., eds. G. Johannes Botterweck and Helmer Ringgren, trans. John T. Wills (Grand Rapids: Eerdmans, 1974), 356.

5. Richard Baxter, *The Practical Works of Richard Baxter in Four Volumes*, vol. 1, *A Christian Directory* (Ligonier, PA: Soli Deo Gloria, 1990), 284.

6. Gregory C. Nichols, "A Biblical View of Anger," ten sermons preached at Trinity Baptist Church, Montville, NJ, Feb.–Mar. 1987. Audiocassettes available from the Trinity Pulpit, Montville, NJ.

7. Leon Morris, *The Cross in the New Testament* (Grand Rapids: Eerdmans, 1965), 149.

8. Elsie Johnson, in *Theological Dictionary*, 356; J. W. Simpson Jr., in *International Standard Bible Encyclopedia*, vol. 4, ed. Geoffrey W. Bromiley (Grand Rapids: Eerdmans, 1988), 1134; H. C. Hahn, "Anger, Wrath; *Orge*," in *New International Dictionary of New Testament Theology*, vol. 1, ed. Colin Brown (Grand Rapids: Zondervan, 1975), 108, 110; Andrew T. Lincoln, *Ephesians*, Word Biblical Commentary Series, vol. 42 (Dallas: Word, 1990), 301; Leslie C. Mitton, *Ephesians*, New Century Bible Series, ed. Matthew Black (London: Marshall, Morgan and Scott, 1976), 168–69.

9. The three Greek New Testament terms are *orge, thymos,* and *aganaktesis,* along with their cognate terms.

10. Richard Walters (1981, 12–13, 28–31), followed by H. Norman Wright (1985, 30–32), presents a tripartite scheme of rage (*thymos*), resentment (*orge*), and indignation *(aganaktesis).*

11. H. C. Hahn, "Anger, Wrath; *Orge*," in *New International Dictionary*, 110; cf. Gustav Stählin, in *Theological Dictionary of the New Testament*, vol. 5, ed. Gerhard Kittel and Gerhard Friedrich, trans. Geoffrey W. Bromiley (Grand Rapids: Eerdmans, 1967), 419.

12. Friedrich Buchsel, in *Theological Dictionary of the New Testament*, vol. 3, ed. Gerhard Kittel and Gerhard Friedrich, trans. Geoffrey W. Bromiley (Grand Rapids: Eerdmans, 1965), 167–68; cf. H. Schonweiss, in *New International Dictionary of New Testament Theology*, vol. 1, ed. Colin Brown (Grand Rapids: Zondervan, 1975), 105–6; H. C. Hahn, "Anger, Wrath; *Orge*," in *New International Dictionary*, 110; Gustav Stählin, in *Theological Dictionary*.

Chapter 2: Is Your Anger Really Righteous?

1. Westminster Shorter Catechism, Q. 14.

2. David A. Powlison, "Anger Part 1: Understanding Anger," *Journal of Biblical Counseling* 14:1 (1995): 48–53.

3. Some writers point to the events in Matthew 23; Luke 13:32; and John 11:33–37.

4. Similar accounts are given in Matthew 21:12–13; Mark 11:15–17; and Luke 19:45–46. Scholars debate whether these reflect one event or two separate events.

5. Benjamin Breckinridge Warfield, "The Emotional Life of Our Lord," in *The Person and Work of Christ* (Phillipsburg, NJ: P&R, 1950), 120–21.

6. B. F. Westcott, *The Gospel According to St. John* (London: John Murray, 1937), en loc.

7. As in the case of our Lord, other Old Testament narrative accounts could be cited. Consider, for instance, the moving example of Phinehas in Numbers 25:1–18 or of Moses in Exodus 32 (mentioned in chapter 1).

8. Saint Augustine, *The Confessions of Saint Augustine* (New Kensington, PA: Whitaker House, 1996), 118.

9. Ibid.

10. Ibid.

11. Ibid.

12. For a discussion of Ephesians 4:26, see Appendix B, where I conclude, along with the vast majority of New Testament Greek scholars, that the imperative is better understood as a concession than as a command.

Chapter 3: Getting to the Heart of Anger

1. Alexander Solzhenitsyn, *One Day in the Life of Ivan Denisovich* (New York: Penguin, 1963), 154.

2. Saint Augustine, *The Confessions of Saint Augustine* (New Kensington, PA: Whitaker House, 1996), 15–20.

3. Ibid., 16.

4. Ibid., 19.

5. Ibid.

6. Ibid.

7. Ibid.

Chapter 4: Repentance: The Road to Uprooting Heart Anger

1. David Powlison, "Biblical Dynamics of Godly Change," D.Min. class lecture, Westminster Theological Seminary, Philadelphia, Aug. 1993.

2. Gregory C. Nichols, "A Biblical View of Anger," ten sermons preached at Trinity Baptist Church, Montville, NJ, Feb.–Mar. 1987.

Chapter 5: Changing Our Angry Behavior: Sinful Revealing

1. Various psychodynamic psychology approaches use "hydraulic" imagery, viewing anger as a kind of fluid or thing. Yet as we saw in chapter 1, anger is not a force that we must ooze or cork or lance or drain, but a human choice, an active judgmental response calling for action. We choose to reveal or conceal that anger in various ways. The revealing/concealing language better addresses the motivational issues behind our angry behavior.

2. Other schemes are possible; there is no limit to how we might slice the empirical pie of angry behavior. And each method would carry value. We could divide angry behavior into offensive (or attacking) and defensive (or retreating) methods. Or the proverbial "fight or flight" options. While not addressing anger per se at this point, Ken Sande of Peacemaker Ministries pictures two wrong kinds of responses to conflicts as "attack responses" and "escape responses." Some angry people strike out at their offenders; others run for safety. The attack need not be overt or ventilating. See Ken Sande, *The Peacemaker: A Biblical Guide to Resolving Personal Conflict*, 3d ed. (Grand Rapids: Baker, 2004), 22–25. In addition, one could classify angry behavior based on the object of that anger: against the offender, against other people or objects ("kick the dog"), or against yourself. Or we could conceive of anger in terms of active, passive, or avoiding behavior. Or one could analyze angry behavior in terms of sins of omission and sins of commission.

3. Ken Sande, *The Peacemaker: A Biblical Guide to Resolving Personal Conflict*, 3d ed. (Grand Rapids: Baker, 2004); Ken Sande

with Tom Raabe, *Peacemaking for Families: A Biblical Guide to Managing Conflict in Your Home* (Wheaton, IL: Tyndale, 2002); Wayne Mack, *Your Family, God's Way: Developing and Sustaining Relationships in the Home* (Phillipsburg, NJ: P&R, 1991).

Chapter 6: Changing Our Angry Behavior: Sinful Concealing

1. This metaphor must not be stretched into a literal geographical notion of so-called inhabiting demons or territorial spirits. Nor does this text justify exorcistic modes of ministry. In keeping with Ephesians 6:10–20, James 4, and 1 Peter 5 (see chapter 4 above), this passage pictures spiritual warfare as resisting the devil by repenting of sinful anger, not by rebuking him or casting out anger demons. See also David A. Powlison, *Power Encounters: Reclaiming Spiritual Warfare* (Grand Rapids: Baker, 1995).

2. Patrick H. Morison, *Forgive! As the Lord Forgave You* (Phillipsburg, NJ: Presbyterian and Reformed, 1977).

3. They are sinful, of course, because God says so in verses such as Proverbs 29:11, not because of "relatively recent research discoveries" (Neil Clark Warren, *Make Anger Your Ally*, 2d ed. [Brentwood, TN: Wolgemuth & Hyatt, 1990], 85–88), although such observations might *illustrate* biblical truth. We are not dependent on sociological or psychological research to determine or even confirm righteous and unrighteous behavior.

4. John Bettler, "Marriage and Family Counseling," D.Min. course lecture, Westminster Theological Seminary, Philadelphia, Aug. 1992; cf. "The Four Rules of Communication," Faith Baptist Counseling Ministries, Lafayetter, IN, Feb. 1994.

5. Wayne Mack, *Your Family, God's Way: Developing and Sustaining Relationships in the Home* (Phillipsburg, NJ: P&R, 1991).

6. Ken Sande, *The Peacemaker: A Biblical Guide to Resolving Personal Conflict*, 3d ed. (Grand Rapids: Baker, 2004), and Ken Sande with Tom Raabe, *Peacemaking for Families: A Biblical Guide to Managing Conflict in Your Home* (Wheaton, IL: Tyndale, 2002).

Chapter 7: Anger against God

1. This chapter was originally published as a booklet in the Resources for Changing Lives Ministry Booklet series: Robert D. Jones, *Angry at God?: Bring Him Your Doubts & Questions* (Phillipsburg, NJ: P&R, 2003).

2. Kay Arthur, "But I'm So Angry!" in *Lord, Heal My Hurts* (Sisters, OR: Multnomah, 1989).

3. John Calvin, *Sermons from Job*, selected and trans. Leroy Nixon (Grand Rapids: Eerdmans, 1952), 29. Emphasis added.

4. Ibid., 29–30. Emphasis added.

5. Ibid., 30. Emphasis added.

6. I recommend Jerry Bridges, *Trusting God: Even When Life Hurts* (Colorado Springs: NavPress, 1988); his booklet-sized abridgment of this, *You Can Trust God* (Colorado Springs: NavPress, 1989); Joni Eareckson Tada and Steven Estes, *When God Weeps: Why Our Sufferings Matter to the Almighty* (Grand Rapids: Zondervan, 1997); and John J. Murray's booklet, *Behind a Frowning Providence* (Carlisle, PA: Banner of Truth, 1990).

Chapter 8: Anger against Yourself

1. Much of this chapter has been adapted from the author's previous booklet, *Forgiveness: "I Just Can't Forgive Myself!"* (Phillipsburg, NJ: P&R, 2003), in the Christian Counseling and Educational Foundation's Resources for Changing Lives Ministry Booklet series.

2. Richard Baxter, *The Practical Works of Richard Baxter*, vol. 1, *A Christian Directory* (Ligonier, PA: Soli Deo Gloria, 1990), 284.

3. John Owen, "The Mortification of Sin in Believers," chap. 2 in William Goold, ed., *The Works of John Owen*, vol. 6 (Edinburgh: Banner of Truth, 1981).

4. I am grateful to David Powlison for suggesting this third point in private correspondence and for his insightful contributions to my earlier writings on this topic.

5. 1 Cor. 4:3–5; James 4:11–12; 1 Peter 2:24; 3:18

Chapter 9: Helping Others Deal with Their Anger

1. Paul David Tripp, *Instruments in the Redeemer's Hands: People in Need of Change Helping People in Need of Change* (Phillipsburg, NJ: P&R, 2002).

2. The following texts all picture the personal ministry of God's truth by not just pastors/elders but all other Christian persons: Romans 15:14; Galatians 6:1–2; Ephesians 4:12–16; Colossians 3:16; 1 Thessalonians 5:12–13; Hebrews 13:12–13; James 5:19–20. Within American evangelicalism, Jay E. Adams pioneered the recovery of biblical counseling by God's people in *Competent to Counsel* (Nutley, NJ: Presbyterian and Reformed, 1970). As his title indicates, Adams persuasively argues that God calls and equips his people to counsel one another. Over the last thirty-five years this movement has grown and developed—in various forms and nuances—through the work of organizations such as the Christian Counseling and Educational Foundation and the National Association of Nouthetic Counselors.

3. For a fuller treatment on how to do personal ministry, be it informal people-helping or formal counseling, read Paul David Tripp, *Instruments in the Redeemer's Hands*. Tripp's four-function framework of "Love, Know, Speak, Do," along with his teaching and our conversations over the years, helped to form my ministry process in this chapter.

4. Jay E. Adams, *Christ and Your Problems* (Nutley, NJ: Presbyterian and Reformed, 1971); Jerry Bridges, *You Can Trust God* (Colorado Springs: NavPress, 1989).

5. John Bettler, "Marriage and Family Counseling," D.Min. course lecture, Westminster Theological Seminary, Philadelphia, Aug. 1992.

6. In some cases I have expanded on this by adding a fill-in for the last statement: "Because you failed, you are bad and I have a right to punish you by *(yelling at you, withdrawing from you, gossiping about you, etc.)*."

7. Ken Sande, *The Peacemaker: A Biblical Guide to Resolving Personal Conflict*, 3d ed. (Grand Rapids: Baker, 2004), chap. 5; Ken Sande with Tom Raabe, *Peacemaking for Families: A Biblical Guide to Managing Conflict in Your Home* (Wheaton, IL: Tyndale, 2002), chap. 2. Sande acknowledges his great debt to John Bettler, David

Powlison, Paul Tripp, and Ed Welch, biblical teachers-counselors from whom I, too, have profited greatly in many years of instruction and conversation.

8. Sande, *The Peacemaker*, 115–16, and *Peacemaking for Families*, 30.

9. Jay Adams, *How to Overcome Evil: A Practical Exposition of Romans 12:14–21* (Nutley, NJ: Presbyterian and Reformed, 1977).

10. Jerry Bridges, *Transforming Grace* (Colorado Springs: Nav-Press, 1991); Patrick Morison, *Forgive! As the Lord Forgave You* (Nutley, NJ: Presbyterian and Reformed, 1977).

11. Jerry Bridges, *Trusting God: Even When Life Hurts* (Colorado Springs: NavPress, 1988); *You Can Trust God*; John J. Murray, *Behind a Frowning Providence* (Carlisle, PA: Banner of Truth, 1990).

12. Jay E. Adams, *From Forgiven to Forgiving* (Amityville, NY: Calvary Press, 1994).

13. Paul David Tripp, *War of Words: Getting to the Heart of Your Communication Struggles* (Phillipsburg, NJ: P&R, 2000) 240–43.

14. Wayne Mack, *Homework Manual for Biblical Living*, vol. 1, *Personal and Interpersonal Problems* (Phillipsburg, NJ: Presbyterian and Reformed, 1979), 1–13. Note: You may need to adapt and shorten these assignments to fit the specific needs of people to whom you minister.

Chapter 10: Why You Must Deal with Your Sinful Anger

1. Richard Baxter, *The Practical Works of Richard Baxter in Four Volumes*, vol. 1, *A Christian Directory* (Ligonier, PA: Soli Deo Gloria, 1990), 284.

2. Frederick Buechner, untitled excerpt in sample issue of Better Families monthly newsletter, ed. J. Allan Petersen, published by Family Concern, Morrison, Colo., 1993.

Appendix A

1. Adapted from Wayne Mack, *Homework Manual for Biblical Living*, vol. 1, *Personal and Interpersonal Problems* (Phillipsburg, NJ: Presbyterian and Reformed, 1979), 4–6, 8.

Appendix B

1. Exceptional views exist, of course. For example, John Calvin, *Sermons on the Epistle to the Ephesians* (orig. 1562; Carlisle, PA: Banner of Truth, 1973), 443–45, understood this imperative as a command to be angry at yourself through self-examination of your own sins. Such self-anger, followed by repentance, will keep you from sinfully holding anger against others. While this insight is true in light of other Scripture (e.g., James 3:13–4:12; Matt. 7:3–5), and powerfully relevant in dealing with anger, this is probably *not* what *this* text intended.

2. R. C. H. Lenski, *The Interpretation of St. Paul's Epistles to the Galatians, to the Ephesians and to the Philippians* (Minneapolis: Augsburg, 1937), 576–77; D. Martyn Lloyd-Jones, *Darkness and Light: An Exposition of Ephesians 4:17–5:17* (Grand Rapids: Baker, 1982), 225–31; John F. MacArthur, "Ephesians," in *The MacArthur New Testament* (Chicago: Moody, 1986), 184–85; S. D. F. Salmond, "The Epistle to the Ephesians," in *The Expositor's Greek Testament*, vol. 3, ed. W. Robertson Nicoll (Grand Rapids: Eerdmans, 1980), 345; Charles R. Swindoll, *Three Steps Forward, Two Steps Back* (Nashville: Thomas Nelson, 1980), 151–53; Kenneth S. Wuest, *Ephesians and Colossians in the Greek New Testament for the English Reader* (Grand Rapids: Eerdmans, 1953), 454; A. Skevington Wood, "Ephesians," in *The Expositor's Bible Commentary*, vol. 11, ed. Frank E. Gaebelein (Grand Rapids: Zondervan, 1978), 64; and apparently T. K. Abbott, *A Critical and Exegetical Commentary on the Epistles to the Ephesians and to the Colossians*, International Critical Commentary on the Holy Scriptures of the Old and New Testaments Series (Edinburgh: T. & T. Clark, 1979), 140; and William Hendricksen, *Exposition of Ephesians*, New Testament Commentary Series, vol. 10 (Grand Rapids: Baker, 1967), 217–18.

3. Henry Alford, *Alford's Greek Testament: An Exegetical and Critical Commentary*, vol. 3 (Grand Rapids: Baker, 1980), 125; Markus Barth, *Ephesians: Translation and Commentary on Chapters 4–6* (Garden City, NY: Doubleday, 1974), 513; Friedrich Blass and Albert Debrunner, *A Greek Grammar of the New Testament*

and Other Early Christian Literature, trans. and rev. Robert F. Funk (Chicago: University of Chicago Press, 1961), 195; Robert G. Bratcher and Eugene A. Nida, *A Translator's Handbook on Paul's Letter to the Ephesians*, Helps for Translators Series (New York: United Bible Societies, 1982), 117; James A. Brooks and Carlton L. Winberry, *Syntax of New Testament Greek* (Washington: University Press of America, 1978), 118; H. C. Hahn, "Anger, Wrath; *Orge*," in *New International Dictionary of New Testament Theology*, vol. 1, ed. Colin Brown (Grand Rapids: Zondervan, 1975), 110; Harold W. Hoehner, "Ephesians," in *The Bible Knowledge Commentary*, vol. 2, New Testament ed. John F. Walvoord and Roy B. Zuck (Wheaton, IL: Victor, 1983), 637; Walter L. Liefeld, "Ephesians," in *The NIV Study Bible*, ed. Kenneth Barker (Grand Rapids: Zondervan, 1985), 1797; Andrew T. Lincoln, *Ephesians*, Word Biblical Commentary Series, vol. 42 (Dallas: Word, 1990), 301; Leslie C. Mitton, *Ephesians*, New Century Bible Series, ed. Matthew Black (London: Marshall, Morgan and Scott, 1976), 168–69; John R. W. Stott, *The Message of Ephesians: God's New Society*, Bible Speaks Today Series (Downers Grove, IL: InterVarsity Press, 1979), 185; David G. Stewart, *The Zondervan Pictorial Encyclopedia of the Bible*, vol. 1, ed. Merril C. Tenney (Grand Rapids: Zondervan, 1975), 167; and apparently F. F. Bruce, *The Epistles to the Colossians, to Philemon, and to the Ephesians*, New International Commentary on the New Testament Series, ed. F. F. Bruce (Grand Rapids: Eerdmans, 1984), 361.

4. Leslie C. Mitton, *Ephesians*, 168.

5. Andrew T. Lincoln, *Ephesians*, 301. Emphasis added.

6. H. C. Hahn, "Anger, Wrath; *Orge*," in *New International Dictionary*, 110. Emphasis added.

7. Wilhelm Michaelis, in *Theological Dictionary of the New Testament*, vol. 6, ed. Gerhard Friedrich (Grand Rapids: Eerdmans, 1971), 990.

8. C. S. Keener, *IVP Biblical Background Commentary: New Testament* (Downers Grove, IL: InterVarsity Press, 1993), 680.

9. David G. Peterson, in *New Bible Commentary: 21st Century Edition*, ed. D. A. Carson (Downers Grove, IL: InterVarsity Press, 1994).

10. Zane Hodges, "Hebrews," in *Bible Knowledge Commentary: An Exposition of the Scriptures*, vol. 2, ed. J. F. Walvoord and R. B. Zuck (Victor Books, 1985), 810, writes, "As a grim reminder of what can happen among believers, the writer warned that one who misses the grace of God may become like a bitter root whose infidelity to God affects others. Here the author had in mind Deut. 29:18 where an Old-Covenant apostate was called a 'root . . . that produces such bitter poison.' " See also David A. DeSilva, *Perseverance in Gratitude: A Socio-Rhetorical Commentary on the Epistle "to the Hebrews"* (Grand Rapids: Eerdmans, 2000), 460; Philip Edgecumbe Hughes, *A Commentary on the Epistle to the Hebrews* (Grand Rapids: Eerdmans, 1977), 538–39; William L. Lane, "Hebrews 9–13," in *Word Biblical Commentary*, vol. 47B (Waco, TX: Word, 1991), 453–54; Paul Ellingworth, "The Epistle to the Hebrews," in *New International Greek Testament Commentary* (Grand Rapids: Eerdmans, 1993), 664; George Guthrie, "Hebrews," in *NIV Application Commentary* (Grand Rapids: Zondervan, 1998), 409. F. F. Bruce, "The Epistle to the Hebrews," in *New International Commentary on the New Testament* (Grand Rapids: Eerdmans, 1964), 365–66, concurs but views the "root' not as the apostate himself but as the apostate's sin. Leon Morris, "Hebrews," in *Expositor's Bible Commentary*, vol. 12, ed. Frank C. Gaebelein (Grand Rapids: Zondervan, 1978), 139–140, agrees that the text warns against apostasy and alludes to Deuteronomy 29:18, but incorrectly (and seemingly alone) sees in the text the actual sin of "bitterness" leading to apostasy.

INDEX OF SCRIPTURE

Robert D. Jones (D.Min, Westminster Theological Seminary; M.Div, Trinity Evangelical Divinity School) is assistant professor of biblical counseling at Southeastern Baptist Theological Seminary. He is the author of the Resources for Changing Lives booklets *Forgiveness*, *Angry at God?* and *Bad Memories*, and has written numerous articles and book reviews for the *Journal of Biblical Counseling*.

Jones is a member of the National Association of Nouthetic Counselors (NANC). He is also a Certified Christian Conciliator and Adjunct Instructor with Peacemaker Ministries (and their Institute for Christian Conciliation), and has served as an adjunct trainer with the Christian Counseling and Educational Foundation (CCEF).

An experienced conference speaker, Jones presents "The Peacemaker Seminar" at local churches and counseling organizations throughout the United States, and in Spain and Brazil. He presents workshops at conferences for NANC and the Biblical Counseling Institute.

Jones live in Raleigh, North Carolina, with his wife and two sons.